Ivan Kushnir

Economy of Andorra

Series "Economy in countries"

first published: 2019
last updated: 2021-01-26

Ivan Kushnir. Economy of Andorra. Series "Economy in countries". - 2019. - 67 pages.

This book about the economy of Andorra from the 1970s to the 2010s. Source data from UN Data.

Size. In the 2010s, the GDP of Andorra was equal to $3.2 billion per year; the value of agriculture was $17.0 million; the value of industry was $152.7 million. Since the share in the world is less than .01%, the country is classified as a micro economy.

Productivity. In the 2010s, the GDP per capita was $39 865.8, the value of agriculture per capita was $213.5, the value of industry per capita was $1 916.1. Since the productivity is greater the average above average, the economy is classified as high developed.

Growth. In the 2010s, the growth of GDP was 0.058%; the growth of agriculture was 2.7%; the growth of industry was 0.73%.

Structure. In the 2010s, the economy of Andorra consisted of: services (56.4%), trade (25.1%), construction (6.9%), transportation (5.6%), industry (5.4%), and agriculture (0.60%).

Exports and imports. In the 2010s, the exports were 7.9% higher than the imports, the net exports were equal to 2.4% of the GDP. The technological structure of exports are better than the structure of imports.

Consumption and reproduction. The attitude of reproduction to the consumption is better than the global average, so the share of GDP in the world will increase.

Series "Economy in countries": parallel.page.link/en

ISBN: 9781794589025

Contents

Part I. Size

	The 2010s
GDP	$3.2 billion
The share in the world	0.0041%
Share in Europe	0.015%
Share in Southern Europe	0.078%

Chapter I. Gross domestic product

The Andorra's gross domestic product increased from $258.1 million per year in the 1970s to $3.2 billion per year in the 2010s, that is by $2.9 billion or 12.3 times. The change occurred at $2.5 billion due to a 4.8-fold increase in prices, as also at -$30.0 million due to a 1.0-fold decrease in productivity, as well as at $431.6 million due to the expansion in population. The average annual growth in GDP is 2.5%. The minimum value of GDP was in 1970 at $99.5 million. The maximum value of gross domestic product was in 2008 at $4.1 billion.

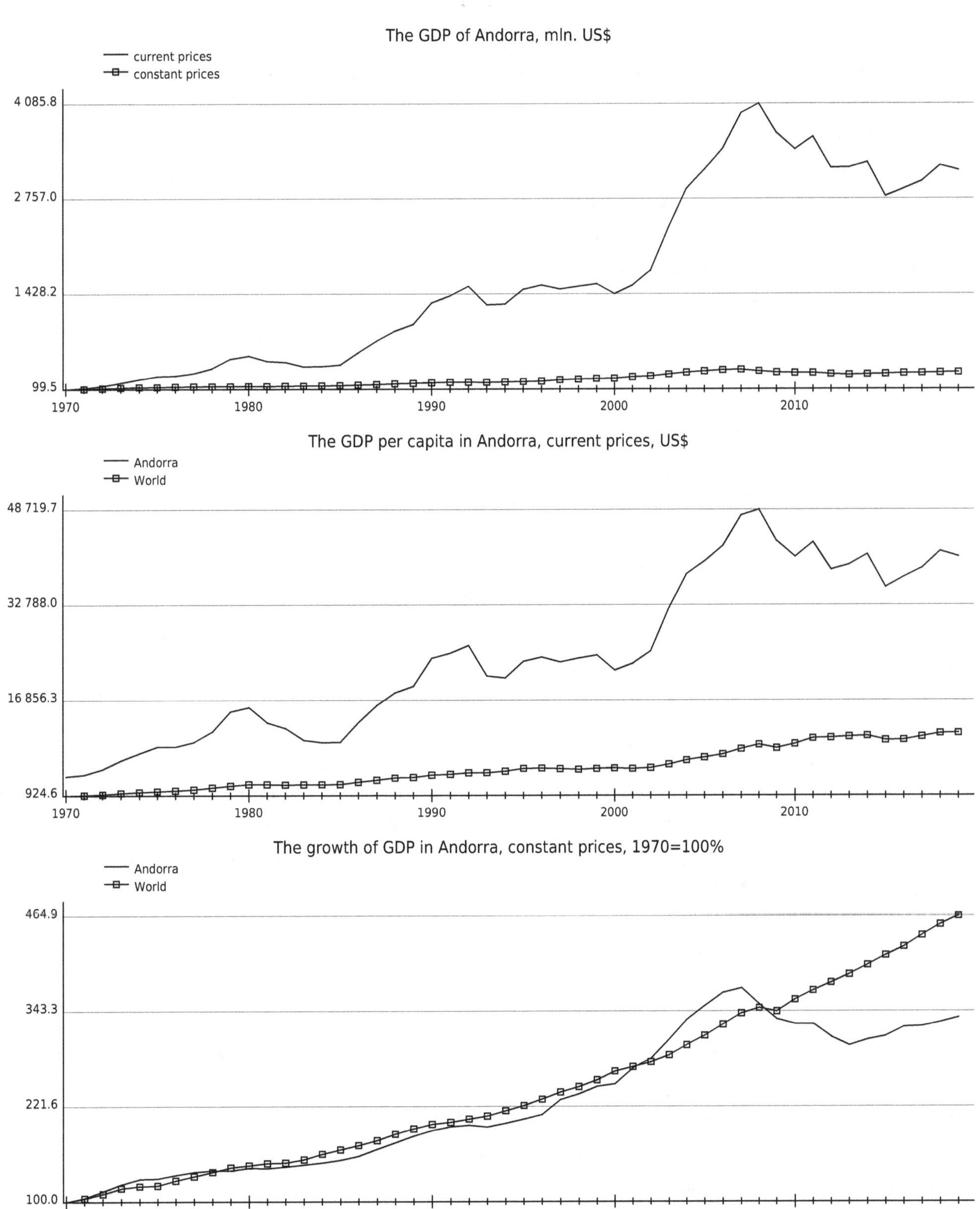

The 1970s

The Andorran GDP was $258.1 million per year in the 1970s, ranked 149th in the world, and was on a par with Aruba ($252.4 million). The share in the world was 0.0039%, and 0.0096% in Europe.

The GDP of Andorra consisted of: household expenditure (64.2%), capital formation (26.9%), and government expenditure (11.5%).

The gross domestic product per capita in Andorra was $8 652.7 in the 1970s, ranked 11th in the world, and was on a par with Bermuda ($8.7 thousand). The GDP per capita in Andorra was greater than gross domestic product per capita in the world ($1 620.8) in 5.3 times, and was greater than GDP per capita in Europe ($3 694.0) in 2.3 times.

The growth of gross domestic product in Andorra was 3.8% in the 1970s, ranked 108th in the world, and was on a par with Sudan (3.8%), Spain (3.8%), Anguilla (3.8%). The growth of GDP in Andorra (3.8%) was less than growth of GDP in the world (4.1%), was greater than growth of GDP in Europe (3.6%).

Comparison with neighbors. The Andorra's GDP was less than in France ($333.2 billion) and in Spain ($106.4 billion). The gross domestic product per capita in Andorra was greater than in France ($6.2 thousand) and in Spain ($3.0 thousand). The growth of GDP in Andorra was greater than in Spain (3.8%); but less than in France (3.9%).

Comparison with leaders. The gross domestic product of Andorra was less than in the United States ($1.7 trillion), in the USSR ($649.4 billion), in Japan ($558.0 billion), in Germany ($484.2 billion), and in France ($333.2 billion). The GDP per capita in Andorra was greater than in the USA ($7.8 thousand), in France ($6.2 thousand), in Germany ($6.1 thousand), in Japan ($5.0 thousand), and in the USSR ($2.6 thousand). The growth of GDP in Andorra was greater than in the USA (3.5%) and in Germany (3.1%); but less than in the USSR (4.8%), in Japan (4.6%), and in France (3.9%).

The 1980s

The gross domestic product of Andorra was $610.7 million per year in the 1980s, ranked 149th in the world. The share in the world was 0.0040%, and 0.011% in Europe.

The GDP of Andorra consisted of: household consumption expenditure (63.3%), capital formation (23.5%), and government consumption expenditure (15.1%).

The Andorra's GDP per capita was $13 919.7 in the 1980s, ranked 21st in the world, and was on a par with Australia ($13.9 thousand), the Bahamas ($14.0 thousand). The Andorran GDP per capita was greater than gross domestic product per capita in the world ($3 123.4) in 4.5 times, and was greater than GDP per capita in Europe ($7 066.6) by 97.0%.

The growth of GDP in Andorra was 2.8% in the 1980s, ranked 97th in the world, and was on a par with Algeria (2.8%), Spain (2.8%). The growth of gross domestic product in Andorra (2.8%) was less than growth of GDP in the world (3.0%), was greater than growth of gross domestic product in Europe (2.5%).

Comparison with neighbors. The Andorran gross domestic product was less than in France ($729.5 billion) and in Spain ($251.6 billion). The gross domestic product per capita in Andorra was greater than in France ($12.9 thousand) and in Spain ($6.5 thousand). The growth of gross domestic product in Andorra was greater than in France (2.3%); but less than in Spain (2.8%).

Comparison with leaders. The Andorran GDP was less than in the United States ($4.2 trillion), in Japan ($1.8 trillion), in Germany ($990.0 billion), in the USSR ($887.0 billion), and in France ($729.5 billion). The gross domestic product per capita in Andorra was greater than in France ($12.9 thousand), in Germany ($12.7 thousand), and in the USSR ($3.2 thousand); but less than in the United States ($17.4 thousand) and in Japan ($15.0 thousand). The growth of GDP in Andorra was greater than in France (2.3%) and in Germany (1.9%); but less than in the USSR (4.3%), in Japan (4.3%), and in the United States (3.1%).

The 1990s

The Andorra's GDP was $1.4 billion per year in the 1990s, ranked 162nd in the world, and was on a par with Laos ($1.5 billion). The share in the world was 0.0050%, and 0.015% in Europe.

The GDP of Andorra consisted of: household expenditure (60.9%), capital formation (23.7%), and public expenditure (17.3%).

The GDP per capita in Andorra was $23 475.5 in the 1990s, ranked 21st in the world, and was on a par with the UK ($22.9 thousand). The GDP per capita in Andorra was greater than gross domestic product per capita in the world ($5 020.1) in 4.7 times, and was greater than GDP per capita in Europe ($13 469.1) by 74.3%.

The growth of GDP in Andorra was 3% in the 1990s, ranked 95th in the world. The growth of GDP in Andorra (3.0%) was greater than growth of GDP in the world (2.8%), was greater than growth of GDP in Europe (1.4%).

Comparison with neighbors. The Andorran GDP was less than in France ($1.4 trillion) and in Spain ($590.1 billion). The Andorra's gross domestic product per capita was greater than in Spain ($14.8 thousand); but less than in France ($24.1 thousand). The growth of GDP in Andorra was greater than in Spain (2.6%) and in France (2.0%).

Comparison with leaders. The Andorra's GDP was less than in the United States ($7.6 trillion), in Japan ($4.3 trillion), in Germany ($2.2 trillion), in France ($1.4 trillion), and in the UK ($1.3 trillion). The GDP per capita in Andorra was greater than in the United Kingdom ($22.9 thousand); but less than in Japan ($34.3 thousand), in the USA ($28.7 thousand), in Germany ($27.0 thousand), and in France ($24.1 thousand). The growth of gross domestic product in Andorra was greater than in the UK (2.3%), in Germany (2.2%), in France (2.0%), and in Japan (1.5%); but less than in the USA (3.2%).

The 2000s

The gross domestic product of Andorra was $2.8 billion per year in the 2000s, ranked 158th in the world. The share in the world was 0.0061%, and 0.018% in Europe.

The GDP of Andorra included: household consumption expenditure (57.9%), capital formation (28.0%), and government consumption expenditure (17.8%).

The GDP per capita in Andorra was $37 109.1 in the 2000s, ranked 20th in the world, and was on a par with Austria ($37.0 thousand), Finland ($37.6 thousand), the UAE ($37.8 thousand). The Andorran gross domestic product per capita was greater than GDP per capita in the world ($7 176.3) in 5.2 times, and was greater than gross domestic product per capita in Europe ($21 115.4) by 75.7%.

The growth of GDP in Andorra was 3% in the 2000s, ranked 134th in the world, and was on a par with Palestine (3.0%), Luxembourg (3.0%), Australasia (3.0%). The growth of GDP in Andorra (3.0%) was greater than growth of GDP in the world (3.0%), was greater than growth of GDP in Europe (1.8%).

Comparison with neighbors. The GDP of Andorra was less than in France ($2.1 trillion) and in Spain ($1.1 trillion). The Andorra's gross domestic product per capita was greater than in France ($33.4 thousand) and in Spain ($24.9 thousand). The growth of GDP in Andorra was greater than in Spain (2.6%) and in France (1.4%).

Comparison with leaders. The Andorran gross domestic product was less than in the USA ($12.6 trillion), in Japan ($4.7 trillion), in Germany ($2.8 trillion), in China ($2.6 trillion), and in the United Kingdom ($2.3 trillion). The Andorran gross domestic product per capita was greater than in Japan ($36.4 thousand), in Germany ($34.0 thousand), and in China ($1 954.1); but less than in the United States ($42.8 thousand) and in the UK ($38.4 thousand). The growth of GDP in Andorra was greater than in the United States (1.9%), in the United Kingdom (1.7%), in Germany (0.73%), and in Japan (0.50%); but less than in China (10.3%).

The 2010s

The Andorra's GDP was $3.2 billion per year in the 2010s, ranked 169th in the world, and was on a par with Curaçao ($3.1 billion). The share in the world was 0.0041%, and 0.015% in Europe.

The gross domestic product of Andorra consisted of: household expenditure (58.5%), public expenditure (19.6%), capital formation (19.5%), and net export (2.4%).

The Andorran GDP per capita was $39 865.8 in the 2010s, ranked 31st in the world, and was on a par with France ($40.5 thousand), the United Arab Emirates ($40.5 thousand), the Virgin Islands ($39.1 thousand). The gross domestic product per capita in Andorra was greater than gross domestic product per capita in the world ($10 603.1) in 3.8 times, and was greater than gross domestic product per capita in Europe ($28 186.8) by 41.4%.

The growth of gross domestic product in Andorra was 0.1% in the 2010s, ranked 192nd in the world. The growth of gross domestic product in Andorra (0.058%) was less than growth of gross domestic product in the world (3.1%), was less than growth of gross domestic product in Europe (1.6%).

Comparison with neighbors. The Andorra's GDP was 845.3 times lower than in France ($2.7 trillion) and 425.0 times lower than in Spain ($1.4 trillion). The Andorran GDP per capita was 38.2% higher than in Spain ($28.8 thousand); but 1.6% lower than in France ($40.5 thousand). The growth of GDP in Andorra was less than in France (1.4%) and in Spain (1.0%).

Comparison with leaders. The Andorran gross domestic product was 5 652.6 times lower than in the United States ($18.0 trillion), 3 306.3 times lower than in China ($10.5 trillion), 1 645.4 times lower than in Japan ($5.2 trillion), 1 152.3 times lower than in Germany ($3.7 trillion), and 870.7 times lower than in the United Kingdom ($2.8 trillion). The gross domestic product per capita in Andorra was 5.3 times higher than in China ($7.5 thousand); but 29.1% lower than in the United States ($56.2 thousand), 10.9% lower than in Germany ($44.7 thousand), 5.5% lower than in the United Kingdom ($42.2 thousand), and 2.5% lower than in Japan ($40.9 thousand). The growth of GDP in Andorra was less than in China (7.7%), in the United States (2.3%), in Germany (1.9%), in the United Kingdom (1.8%), and in Japan (1.3%).

Chapter II. Value added

The value added of Andorra increased from $215.3 million per year in the 1970s to $2.8 billion per year in the 2010s, that is by $2.6 billion or 13.2 times. The change occurred at $2.2 billion due to a 4.8-fold increase in prices, as also at $13.1 million due to a 1.0-fold increase in productivity, as well as at $360.0 million due to the increase in population. The average annual growth in value added is 2.6%. The minimum value of value added was in 1970 at $83.0 million. The maximum value of value added was in 2008 at $3.7 billion.

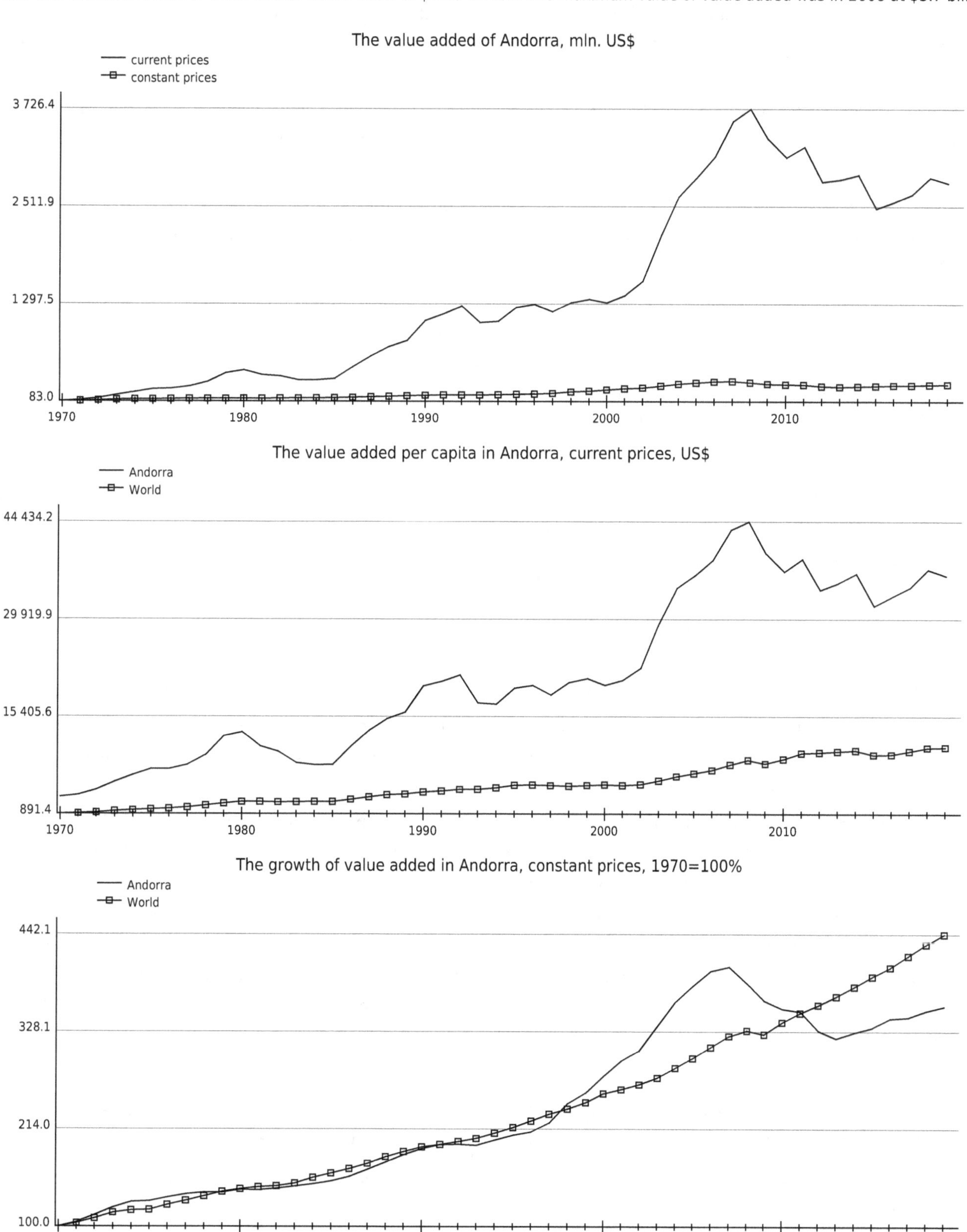

The 1970s

The value added of Andorra was $215.3 million per year in the 1970s, ranked 151st in the world. The share in the world was 0.0034%, and 0.0085% in Europe.

The total value added of Andorra included: trade (40.6%), services (36.9%), construction (11.7%), industry (6.6%), transportation (3.7%), and agriculture (0.48%).

The Andorran value added per capita was $7 218.4 in the 1970s, ranked 12th in the world, and was on a par with Luxembourg ($7.2 thousand). The Andorran value added per capita was greater than value added per capita in the world ($1 564.4) in 4.6 times, and was greater than value added per capita in Europe ($3 506.2) in 2.1 times.

The growth of value added in Andorra was 3.8% in the 1970s, ranked 112th in the world, and was on a par with Iran (3.8%), Canada (3.8%), Dominica (3.8%). The growth of value added in Andorra (3.8%) was less than growth of value added in the world (3.9%), was greater than growth of value added in Europe (3.4%).

Comparison with neighbors. The Andorran value added was less than in France ($297.3 billion) and in Spain ($100.2 billion). The Andorran value added per capita was greater than in France ($5.5 thousand) and in Spain ($2.8 thousand). The growth of value added in Andorra was greater than in France (3.7%); but less than in Spain (4.0%).

Comparison with leaders. The value added of Andorra was less than in the USA ($1.7 trillion), in the USSR ($649.4 billion), in Japan ($545.3 billion), in Germany ($444.9 billion), and in France ($297.3 billion). The value added per capita in Andorra was greater than in Germany ($5.7 thousand), in France ($5.5 thousand), in Japan ($4.9 thousand), and in the USSR ($2.6 thousand); but less than in the USA ($7.8 thousand). The growth of value added in Andorra was greater than in France (3.7%), in Germany (3.1%), and in the United States (2.9%); but less than in Japan (4.9%) and in the USSR (4.8%).

The 1980s

The Andorran value added was $509.4 million per year in the 1980s, ranked 150th in the world. The share in the world was 0.0035%, and 0.0100% in Europe.

The total value added of Andorra consisted of: trade (40.5%), services (36.9%), construction (11.7%), industry (6.6%), transportation (3.7%), and agriculture (0.48%).

The Andorra's value added per capita was $11 611.9 in the 1980s, ranked 25th in the world, and was on a par with Germany ($11.6 thousand), France ($11.5 thousand), Greenland ($11.7 thousand). The value added per capita in Andorra was greater than value added per capita in the world ($3 029.9) in 3.8 times, and was greater than value added per capita in Europe ($6 647.9) by 74.7%.

The growth of value added in Andorra was 2.8% in the 1980s, ranked 95th in the world, and was on a par with Northern Europe (2.8%), Israel (2.8%), Spain (2.8%). The growth of value added in Andorra (2.8%) was less than growth of value added in the world (2.9%), was greater than growth of value added in Europe (2.6%).

Comparison with neighbors. The value added of Andorra was less than in France ($650.9 billion) and in Spain ($236.5 billion). The Andorran value added per capita was greater than in France ($11.5 thousand) and in Spain ($6.1 thousand). The growth of value added in Andorra was greater than in Spain (2.8%) and in France (2.2%).

Comparison with leaders. The value added of Andorra was less than in the USA ($4.2 trillion), in Japan ($1.8 trillion), in Germany ($907.0 billion), in the USSR ($887.0 billion), and in France ($650.9 billion). The Andorra's value added per capita was greater than in France ($11.5 thousand) and in the USSR ($3.2 thousand); but less than in the USA ($17.4 thousand), in Japan ($14.8 thousand), and in Germany ($11.6 thousand). The growth of value added in Andorra was greater than in France (2.2%) and in Germany (2.0%); but less than in the USSR (4.3%), in Japan (4.2%), and in the USA (2.8%).

The 1990s

The Andorran value added was $1.2 billion per year in the 1990s, ranked 166th in the world, and was on a par with the Central African Republic ($1.2 billion), Somalia ($1.2 billion). The share in the world was 0.0044%, and 0.014% in Europe.

The total value added of Andorra included: trade (40.2%), services (37.4%), construction (11.7%), industry (6.5%), transportation (3.7%), and agriculture (0.45%).

The value added per capita in Andorra was $19 650.9 in the 1990s, ranked 27th in the world, and was on a par with Singapore ($19.7

thousand), Canada ($19.7 thousand), Italy ($19.3 thousand). The Andorra's value added per capita was greater than value added per capita in the world ($4 799.9) in 4.1 times, and was greater than value added per capita in Europe ($12 269.4) by 60.2%.

The growth of value added in Andorra was 3.4% in the 1990s, ranked 88th in the world. The growth of value added in Andorra (3.4%) was greater than growth of value added in the world (2.7%), was greater than growth of value added in Europe (1.3%).

Comparison with neighbors. The Andorra's value added was less than in France ($1.3 trillion) and in Spain ($546.8 billion). The value added per capita in Andorra was greater than in Spain ($13.8 thousand); but less than in France ($21.6 thousand). The growth of value added in Andorra was greater than in Spain (2.2%) and in France (1.8%).

Comparison with leaders. The value added of Andorra was less than in the United States ($7.6 trillion), in Japan ($4.3 trillion), in Germany ($2.0 trillion), in France ($1.3 trillion), and in the United Kingdom ($1.2 trillion). The value added per capita in Andorra was less than in Japan ($34.2 thousand), in the United States ($28.6 thousand), in Germany ($24.5 thousand), in France ($21.6 thousand), and in the UK ($21.4 thousand). The growth of value added in Andorra was greater than in the United States (2.8%), in the UK (2.4%), in Germany (2.1%), in France (1.8%), and in Japan (1.8%).

The 2000s

The Andorra's value added was $2.6 billion per year in the 2000s, ranked 159th in the world, and was on a par with Eswatini ($2.6 billion). The share in the world was 0.0058%, and 0.019% in Europe.

The total value added of Andorra consisted of: services (50.5%), trade (27.2%), construction (12.0%), industry (5.0%), transportation (4.8%), and agriculture (0.44%).

The value added per capita in Andorra was $33 721.9 in the 2000s, ranked 21st in the world, and was on a par with Kuwait ($34.3 thousand), Northern Europe ($34.4 thousand), Austria ($33.0 thousand). The value added per capita in Andorra was greater than value added per capita in the world ($6 818.0) in 4.9 times, and was greater than value added per capita in Europe ($18 944.1) by 78.0%.

The growth of value added in Andorra was 3.6% in the 2000s, ranked 107th in the world, and was on a par with Oman (3.6%), Cyprus (3.6%). The growth of value added in Andorra (3.6%) was greater than growth of value added in the world (2.9%), was greater than growth of value added in Europe (1.7%).

Comparison with neighbors. The value added of Andorra was less than in France ($1.9 trillion) and in Spain ($991.9 billion). The value added per capita in Andorra was greater than in France ($30.0 thousand) and in Spain ($22.7 thousand). The growth of value added in Andorra was greater than in Spain (2.7%) and in France (1.4%).

Comparison with leaders. The value added of Andorra was less than in the USA ($12.6 trillion), in Japan ($4.7 trillion), in China ($2.6 trillion), in Germany ($2.5 trillion), and in the United Kingdom ($2.1 trillion). The value added per capita in Andorra was greater than in Germany ($30.7 thousand) and in China ($1 954.1); but less than in the United States ($42.8 thousand), in Japan ($36.4 thousand), and in the United Kingdom ($34.6 thousand). The growth of value added in Andorra was greater than in the United States (1.7%), in the UK (1.7%), in Germany (0.65%), and in Japan (0.27%); but less than in China (10.2%).

The 2010s

The value added of Andorra was $2.8 billion per year in the 2010s, ranked 170th in the world, and was on a par with Curaçao ($2.8 billion). The share in the world was 0.0038%, and 0.015% in Europe.

The total value added of Andorra consisted of: services (56.4%), trade (25.1%), construction (6.9%), transportation (5.6%), industry (5.4%), and agriculture (0.60%).

The value added per capita in Andorra was $35 570.4 in the 2010s, ranked 34th in the world, and was on a par with Israel ($35.0 thousand), France ($36.2 thousand). The Andorra's value added per capita was greater than value added per capita in the world ($10 094.6) in 3.5 times, and was greater than value added per capita in Europe ($25 251.2) by 40.9%.

The growth of value added in Andorra was -0.2% in the 2010s, ranked 196th in the world. The growth of value added in Andorra (-0.19%) was less than growth of value added in the world (3.1%), was less than growth of value added in Europe (1.6%).

Comparison with neighbors. The value added of Andorra was 847.8 times lower than in France ($2.4 trillion) and 434.4 times lower than in Spain ($1.2 trillion). The value added per capita in Andorra was 35.2% higher than in Spain ($26.3 thousand); but 1.8% lower than in France ($36.2 thousand). The growth of value added in Andorra was less than in France (1.3%) and in Spain (0.99%).

Comparison with leaders. The value added of Andorra was 6 335.2 times lower than in the USA ($18.0 trillion), 3 705.5 times lower than in China ($10.5 trillion), 1 834.6 times lower than in Japan ($5.2 trillion), 1 164.9 times lower than in Germany ($3.3 trillion), and 871.3 times lower than in the UK ($2.5 trillion). The Andorra's value added per capita was 4.7 times higher than in China ($7.5 thousand); but 36.7% lower than in the USA ($56.2 thousand), 12.5% lower than in Japan ($40.7 thousand), 11.8% lower than in Germany ($40.3 thousand), and 5.5% lower than in the UK ($37.7 thousand). The growth of value added in Andorra was less than in China (7.7%), in the United States (2.2%), in Germany (1.9%), in the United Kingdom (1.8%), and in Japan (1.3%).

Chapter III. Gross national income

The Andorran gross national income increased from $258.1 million per year in the 1970s to $3.2 billion per year in the 2010s, that is by $2.9 billion or 12.3 times. The change occurred at $2.5 billion due to a 4.8-fold increase in prices, as also at -$30.0 million due to a 1.0-fold decrease in productivity, as well as at $431.6 million due to the increase in population. The average annual growth in gross national income is 2.5%. The minimum value of gross national income was in 1970 at $99.5 million. The maximum value of gross national income was in 2008 at $4.1 billion.

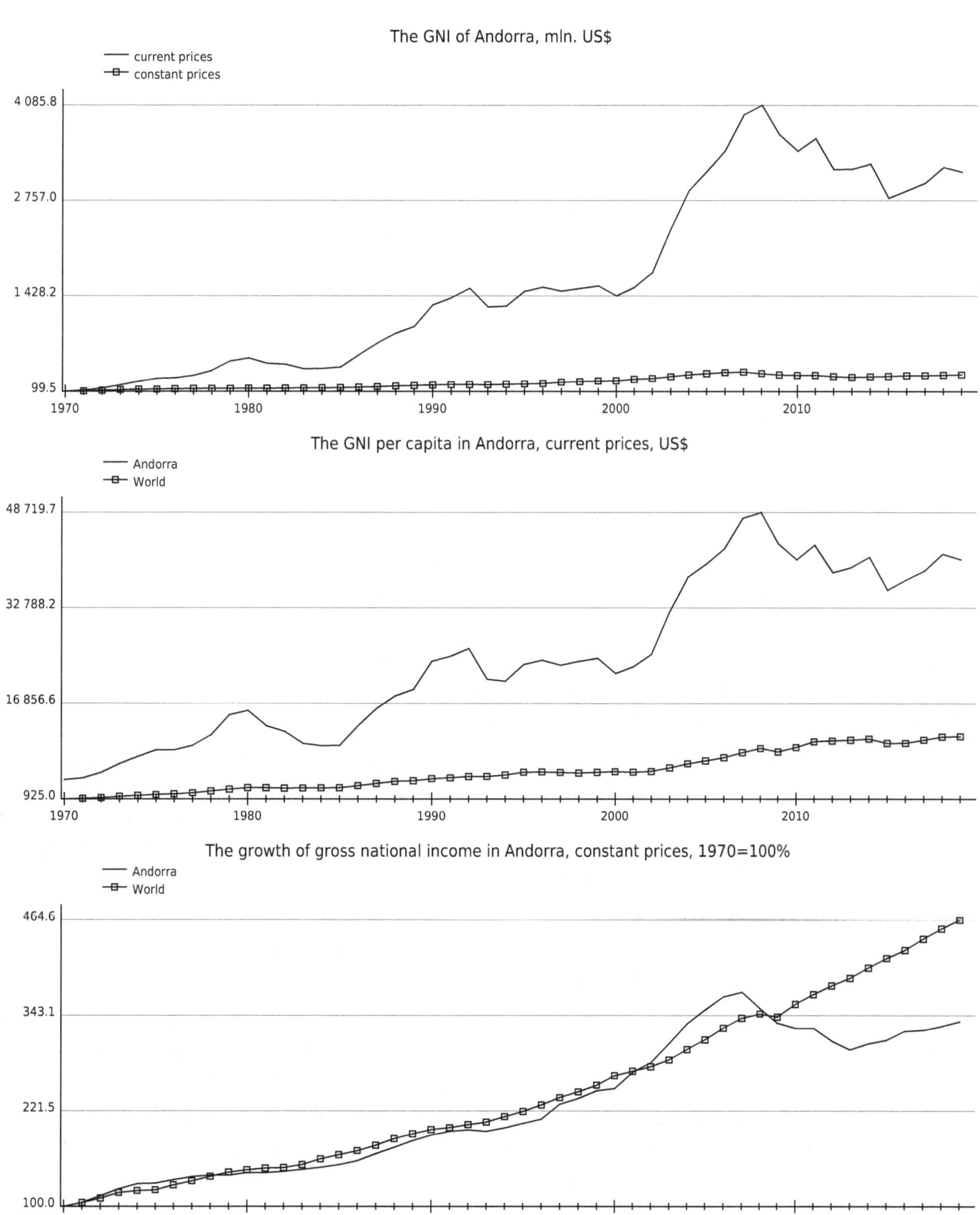

The GNI of Andorra, mln. US$

The GNI per capita in Andorra, current prices, US$

The growth of gross national income in Andorra, constant prices, 1970=100%

The 1970s

The Andorran GNI was $258.1 million per year in the 1970s, ranked 148th in the world, and was on a par with Swaziland ($256.8 million), Botswana ($252.6 million). The share in the world was 0.0039%, and 0.0095% in Europe.

The gross national income per capita in Andorra was $8 652.7 in the 1970s, ranked 10th in the world. The Andorran gross national income per capita was greater than GNI per capita in the world ($1 624.3) in 5.3 times, and was greater than gross national income per capita in Europe ($3 730.2) in 2.3 times.

The growth of gross national income in Andorra was 3.8% in the 1970s, ranked 112th in the world, and was on a par with Austria (3.8%), Anguilla (3.8%), Italy (3.8%). The growth of gross national income in Andorra (3.8%) was less than growth of GNI in the world (4.1%), was greater than growth of GNI in Europe (3.6%).

Comparison with neighbors. The Andorran GNI was less than in France ($334.3 billion) and in Spain ($105.3 billion). The GNI per capita in Andorra was greater than in France ($6.2 thousand) and in Spain ($3.0 thousand). The growth of gross national income in Andorra was less than in France (3.9%) and in Spain (3.8%).

Comparison with leaders. The gross national income of Andorra was less than in the United States ($1.7 trillion), in the USSR ($649.4 billion), in Japan ($558.5 billion), in Germany ($486.2 billion), and in France ($334.3 billion). The GNI per capita in Andorra was greater than in the USA ($7.8 thousand), in France ($6.2 thousand), in Germany ($6.2 thousand), in Japan ($5.0 thousand), and in the USSR ($2.6 thousand). The growth of GNI in Andorra was greater than in the United States (3.5%) and in Germany (3.0%); but less than in the USSR (4.8%), in Japan (4.7%), and in France (3.9%).

The 1980s

The Andorra's gross national income was $610.7 million per year in the 1980s, ranked 149th in the world. The share in the world was 0.0041%, and 0.011% in Europe.

The Andorra's GNI per capita was $13 919.7 in the 1980s, ranked 20th in the world, and was on a par with Australia ($13.7 thousand), Finland ($14.3 thousand). The Andorra's gross national income per capita was greater than GNI per capita in the world ($3 117.1) in 4.5 times, and was greater than GNI per capita in Europe ($7 107.7) by 95.8%.

The growth of GNI in Andorra was 2.8% in the 1980s, ranked 97th in the world, and was on a par with Namibia (2.8%), Spain (2.8%), the Americas (2.8%). The growth of GNI in Andorra (2.8%) was less than growth of GNI in the world (3.0%), was greater than growth of gross national income in Europe (2.4%).

Comparison with neighbors. The gross national income of Andorra was less than in France ($732.1 billion) and in Spain ($247.9 billion). The Andorran gross national income per capita was greater than in France ($13.0 thousand) and in Spain ($6.4 thousand). The growth of GNI in Andorra was greater than in Spain (2.8%) and in France (2.3%).

Comparison with leaders. The Andorran GNI was less than in the USA ($4.2 trillion), in Japan ($1.8 trillion), in Germany ($996.5 billion), in the USSR ($887.0 billion), and in France ($732.1 billion). The GNI per capita in Andorra was greater than in France ($13.0 thousand), in Germany ($12.8 thousand), and in the USSR ($3.2 thousand); but less than in the USA ($17.4 thousand) and in Japan ($15.0 thousand). The growth of gross national income in Andorra was greater than in France (2.3%) and in Germany (2.0%); but less than in Japan (4.4%), in the USSR (4.3%), and in the United States (3.1%).

The 1990s

The gross national income of Andorra was $1.4 billion per year in the 1990s, ranked 161st in the world, and was on a par with Laos ($1.5 billion), Lesotho ($1.4 billion). The share in the world was 0.0051%, and 0.015% in Europe.

The gross national income per capita in Andorra was $23 475.5 in the 1990s, ranked 21st in the world, and was on a par with Finland ($23.5 thousand), the UK ($23.0 thousand). The gross national income per capita in Andorra was greater than gross national income per capita in the world ($4 991.4) in 4.7 times, and was greater than gross national income per capita in Europe ($13 437.3) by 74.7%.

The growth of GNI in Andorra was 3% in the 1990s, ranked 97th in the world, and was on a par with Vanuatu (3.0%). The growth of gross national income in Andorra (3.0%) was greater than growth of GNI in the world (2.8%), was greater than growth of GNI in Europe (1.3%).

Comparison with neighbors. The gross national income of Andorra was less than in France ($1.4 trillion) and in Spain ($583.1 billion).

The Andorra's gross national income per capita was greater than in Spain ($14.7 thousand); but less than in France ($24.3 thousand). The growth of gross national income in Andorra was greater than in Spain (2.7%) and in France (2.2%).

Comparison with leaders. The GNI of Andorra was less than in the United States ($7.5 trillion), in Japan ($4.4 trillion), in Germany ($2.2 trillion), in France ($1.4 trillion), and in the UK ($1.3 trillion). The Andorran GNI per capita was greater than in the UK ($23.0 thousand); but less than in Japan ($34.7 thousand), in the United States ($28.5 thousand), in Germany ($27.0 thousand), and in France ($24.3 thousand). The growth of gross national income in Andorra was greater than in France (2.2%), in the UK (2.0%), in Germany (2.0%), and in Japan (1.5%); but less than in the United States (3.4%).

The 2000s

The GNI of Andorra was $2.8 billion per year in the 2000s, ranked 159th in the world. The share in the world was 0.0061%, and 0.018% in Europe.

The Andorran gross national income per capita was $37 109.1 in the 2000s, ranked 21st in the world, and was on a par with Japan ($37.1 thousand), Austria ($36.9 thousand), Finland ($37.8 thousand). The GNI per capita in Andorra was greater than GNI per capita in the world ($7 165.2) in 5.2 times, and was greater than gross national income per capita in Europe ($21 073.1) by 76.1%.

The growth of gross national income in Andorra was 3% in the 2000s, ranked 131st in the world, and was on a par with Eswatini (3.0%), Mauritania (3.1%). The growth of gross national income in Andorra (3.0%) was greater than growth of GNI in the world (3.0%), was greater than growth of gross national income in Europe (1.8%).

Comparison with neighbors. The Andorra's GNI was less than in France ($2.1 trillion) and in Spain ($1.1 trillion). The gross national income per capita in Andorra was greater than in France ($34.0 thousand) and in Spain ($24.5 thousand). The growth of gross national income in Andorra was greater than in Spain (2.5%) and in France (1.5%).

Comparison with leaders. The Andorran GNI was less than in the USA ($12.7 trillion), in Japan ($4.8 trillion), in Germany ($2.8 trillion), in China ($2.6 trillion), and in the UK ($2.3 trillion). The gross national income per capita in Andorra was greater than in Germany ($34.2 thousand) and in China ($1 950.5); but less than in the United States ($43.2 thousand), in the UK ($38.5 thousand), and in Japan ($37.1 thousand). The growth of gross national income in Andorra was greater than in the USA (1.8%), in the UK (1.7%), in Germany (1.0%), and in Japan (0.62%); but less than in China (10.4%).

The 2010s

The gross national income of Andorra was $3.2 billion per year in the 2010s, ranked 170th in the world, and was on a par with East Timor ($3.2 billion), Curaçao ($3.1 billion). The share in the world was 0.0041%, and 0.015% in Europe.

The GNI per capita in Andorra was $39 865.8 in the 2010s, ranked 31st in the world, and was on a par with New Zealand ($39.3 thousand), the UAE ($40.6 thousand). The GNI per capita in Andorra was greater than gross national income per capita in the world ($10 611.7) in 3.8 times, and was greater than gross national income per capita in Europe ($28 141.7) by 41.7%.

The growth of GNI in Andorra was 0.1% in the 2010s, ranked 193rd in the world. The growth of gross national income in Andorra (0.058%) was less than growth of gross national income in the world (3.1%), was less than growth of gross national income in Europe (1.6%).

Comparison with neighbors. The Andorran GNI was 864.2 times lower than in France ($2.7 trillion) and 423.0 times lower than in Spain ($1.3 trillion). The gross national income per capita in Andorra was 38.9% higher than in Spain ($28.7 thousand); but 3.7% lower than in France ($41.4 thousand). The growth of gross national income in Andorra was less than in France (1.4%) and in Spain (1.2%).

Comparison with leaders. The Andorra's gross national income was 5 761.1 times lower than in the United States ($18.3 trillion), 3 294.1 times lower than in China ($10.5 trillion), 1 699.1 times lower than in Japan ($5.4 trillion), 1 179.9 times lower than in Germany ($3.7 trillion), and 864.2 times lower than in France ($2.7 trillion). The Andorran gross national income per capita was 5.3 times higher than in China ($7.5 thousand); but 30.4% lower than in the USA ($57.3 thousand), 13.0% lower than in Germany ($45.8 thousand), 5.5% lower than in Japan ($42.2 thousand), and 3.7% lower than in France ($41.4 thousand). The growth of GNI in Andorra was less than in China (7.7%), in the United States (2.5%), in Germany (2.0%), in Japan (1.4%), and in France (1.4%).

Part II. Structure

	The 2010s
agriculture	0.60%
industry	5.4%
construction	6.9%
trade	25.1%
transportation	5.6%
services	56.4%

Chapter IV. Agriculture

Agriculture, hunting, forestry, fishing (ISIC A-B)

The agriculture of Andorra grew up from $1.0 million per year in the 1970s to $17.0 million per year in the 2010s, that is by $16.0 million or 16.6 times. The change occurred at $13.5 million due to a 4.8-fold increase in prices, as also at $795.0 thousand due to a 1.3-fold increase in productivity, as well as at $1.7 million due to the rise in population. The average annual growth in agriculture is 3.2%. The minimum value of agriculture was in 1970 at $395.3 thousand. The maximum value of agriculture was in 2012 at $19.2 million.

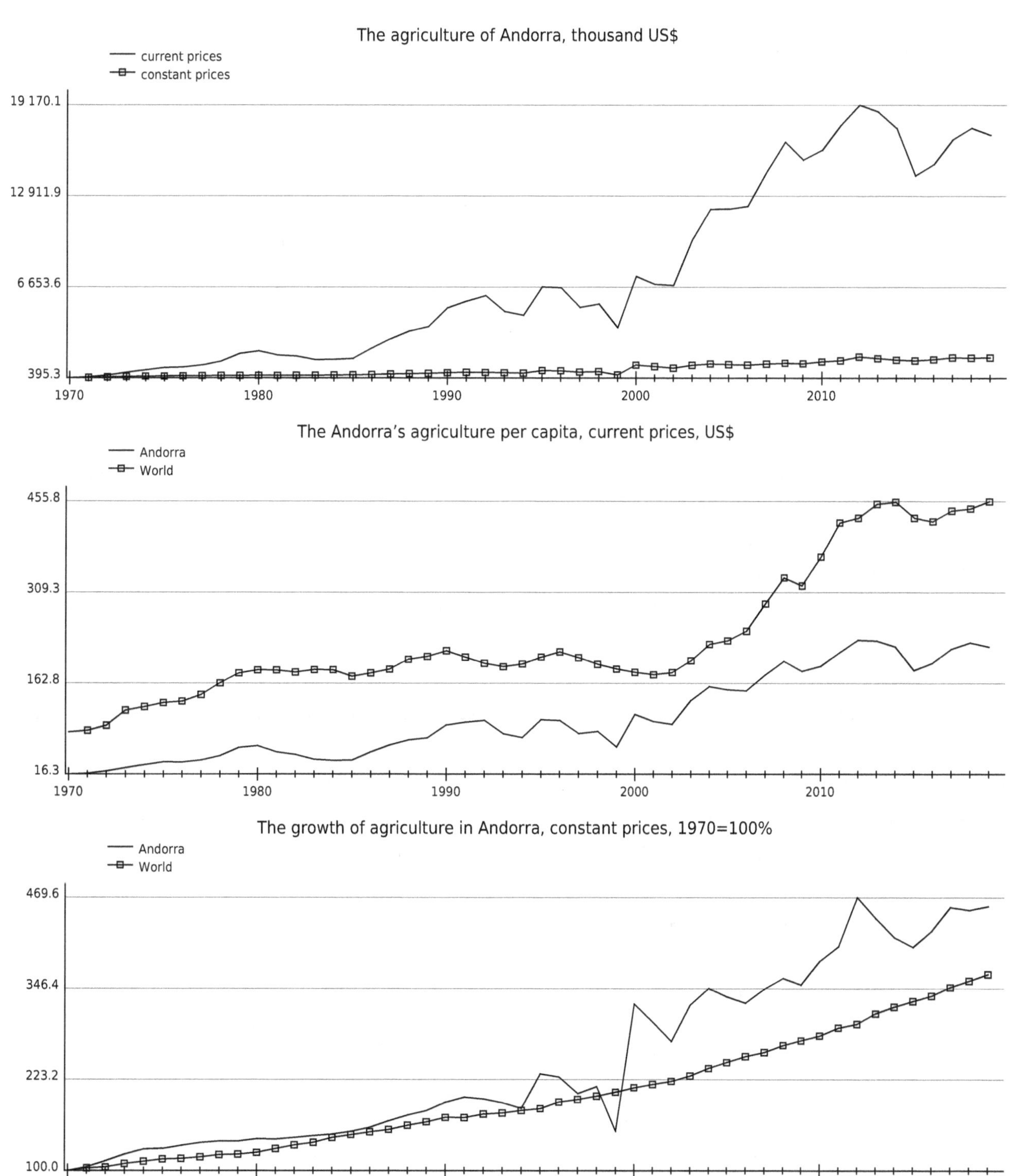

The agriculture of Andorra, thousand US$

The Andorra's agriculture per capita, current prices, US$

The growth of agriculture in Andorra, constant prices, 1970=100%

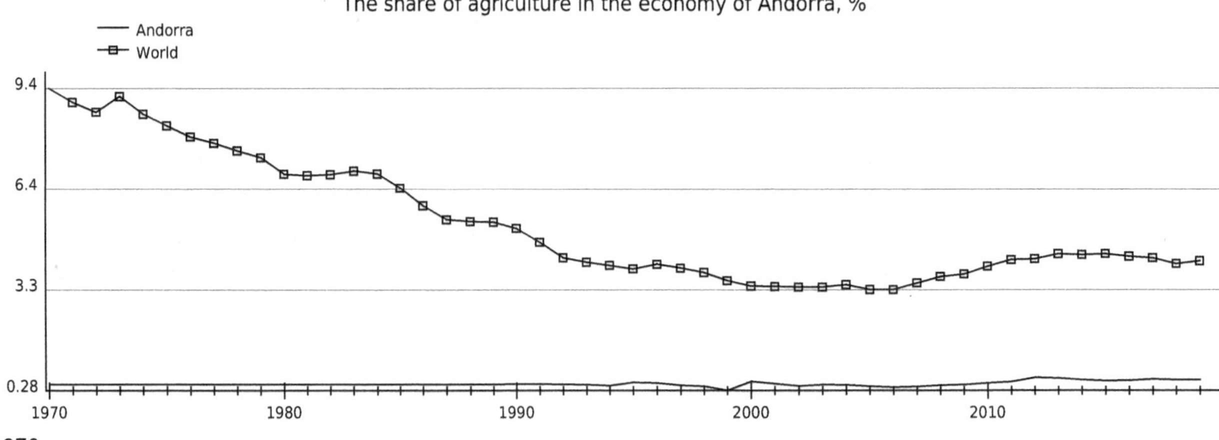

The 1970s

The Andorra's agriculture was $1.0 million per year in the 1970s, ranked 175th in the world. The share in the world was 0.0002%, and 0.0005% in Europe.

The share of agriculture in the economy of Andorra was 0.48% in the 1970s, ranked 178th in the world.

The value added of agriculture per capita in Andorra was $34.4 in the 1970s, ranked 171st in the world. The value of agriculture per capita in Andorra was less than agriculture per capita in the world ($127.6) in 3.7 times, and was less than agriculture per capita in Europe ($268.3) in 7.8 times.

The growth of agriculture in Andorra was 3.8% in the 1970s, ranked 66th in the world, and was on a par with Qatar (3.8%). The growth of agriculture in Andorra (3.8%) was greater than growth of agriculture in the world (2.2%), was greater than growth of agriculture in Europe (3.3%).

Comparison with neighbors. The sector of agriculture in Andorra was less than in France ($16.6 billion) and in Spain ($8.7 billion). The value added of agriculture per capita in Andorra was less than in France ($310.2) and in Spain ($245.2). The growth of agriculture in Andorra was greater than in France (2.8%) and in Spain (2.6%).

Comparison with leaders. The value of agriculture in Andorra was less than in the USSR ($88.7 billion), in China ($49.5 billion), in the USA ($42.6 billion), in India ($36.0 billion), and in Japan ($25.8 billion). The agriculture per capita in Andorra was less than in the USSR ($351.8), in Japan ($231.3), in the United States ($195.0), in India ($58.3), and in China ($54.2). The growth of agriculture in Andorra was greater than in China (2.4%), in Japan (0.52%), in the USA (0.34%), and in India (0.30%); but less than in the USSR (7.0%).

The 1980s

The value of agriculture in Andorra was $2.4 million per year in the 1980s, ranked 174th in the world. The share in the world was 0.0003%, and 0.0008% in Europe.

The share of agriculture in the economy of Andorra was 0.48% in the 1980s, ranked 178th in the world.

The Andorran agriculture per capita was $55.2 in the 1980s, ranked 173rd in the world. The Andorran agriculture per capita was less than agriculture per capita in the world ($186.6) in 3.4 times, and was less than agriculture per capita in Europe ($386.3) in 7.0 times.

The growth of agriculture in Andorra was 2.6% in the 1980s, ranked 85th in the world, and was on a par with Uganda (2.6%), Guinea (2.6%), Zimbabwe (2.6%). The growth of agriculture in Andorra (2.6%) was less than growth of agriculture in the world (3.1%), was greater than growth of agriculture in Europe (2.1%).

Comparison with neighbors. The Andorran agriculture was less than in France ($24.2 billion) and in Spain ($13.5 billion). The value added of agriculture per capita in Andorra was less than in France ($428.2) and in Spain ($350.5). The growth of agriculture in Andorra was greater than in Spain (2.4%) and in France (2.1%).

Comparison with leaders. The sector of agriculture in Andorra was less than in the USSR ($125.8 billion), in China ($94.9 billion), in India ($70.4 billion), in the United States ($68.7 billion), and in Japan ($49.7 billion). The agriculture per capita in Andorra was less than in the USSR ($457.2), in Japan ($410.0), in the United States ($286.8), in India ($90.7), and in China ($88.5). The growth of agriculture in Andorra was greater than in Japan (0.41%); but less than in China (5.3%), in India (4.4%), in the USA (3.7%), and in the

USSR (2.8%).

The 1990s

The Andorran agriculture was $5.5 million per year in the 1990s, ranked 196th in the world. The share in the world was 0.0005%, and 0.0020% in Europe.

The share of agriculture in the economy of Andorra was 0.45% in the 1990s, ranked 199th in the world.

The Andorran agriculture per capita was $88.7 in the 1990s, ranked 180th in the world. The agriculture per capita in Andorra was less than agriculture per capita in the world ($199.8) in 2.3 times, and was less than agriculture per capita in Europe ($382.2) in 4.3 times.

The growth of agriculture in Andorra was -1.7% in the 1990s, ranked 169th in the world. The growth of agriculture in Andorra (-1.7%) was less than growth of agriculture in the world (2.2%), was less than growth of agriculture in Europe (-1.6%).

Comparison with neighbors. The value added of agriculture in Andorra was less than in France ($35.4 billion) and in Spain ($24.8 billion). The value of agriculture per capita in Andorra was less than in Spain ($623.0) and in France ($595.9). The growth of agriculture in Andorra was less than in Spain (3.0%) and in France (2.4%).

Comparison with leaders. The sector of agriculture in Andorra was less than in China ($139.0 billion), in the USA ($96.1 billion), in India ($91.4 billion), in Japan ($78.9 billion), and in Brazil ($36.8 billion). The value added of agriculture per capita in Andorra was less than in Japan ($625.5), in the United States ($363.4), in Brazil ($228.7), in China ($112.7), and in India ($95.6). The growth of agriculture in Andorra was greater than in Japan (-1.8%); but less than in China (4.3%), in Brazil (3.0%), in India (2.8%), and in the United States (2.6%).

The 2000s

The sector of agriculture in Andorra was $11.4 million per year in the 2000s, ranked 194th in the world. The share in the world was 0.0007%, and 0.0040% in Europe.

The share of agriculture in the economy of Andorra was 0.44% in the 2000s, ranked 197th in the world.

The agriculture per capita in Andorra was $149.1 in the 2000s, ranked 149th in the world, and was on a par with the Central African Republic ($148.4), Mali ($150.5), Laos ($150.7). The value added of agriculture per capita in Andorra was less than agriculture per capita in the world ($240.3) by 38.0%, and was less than agriculture per capita in Europe ($387.0) in 2.6 times.

The growth of agriculture in Andorra was 8.7% in the 2000s, ranked 7th in the world, and was on a par with Myanmar (8.6%). The growth of agriculture in Andorra (8.7%) was greater than growth of agriculture in the world (3.0%), was greater than growth of agriculture in Europe (1.2%).

Comparison with neighbors. The value of agriculture in Andorra was less than in France ($35.5 billion) and in Spain ($30.6 billion). The sector of agriculture per capita in Andorra was less than in Spain ($700.2) and in France ($565.3). The growth of agriculture in Andorra was greater than in France (0.86%) and in Spain (0.58%).

Comparison with leaders. The agriculture of Andorra was less than in China ($297.7 billion), in India ($147.6 billion), in the United States ($122.5 billion), in Japan ($57.1 billion), and in Nigeria ($47.6 billion). The agriculture per capita in Andorra was greater than in India ($129.7); but less than in Japan ($445.6), in the USA ($416.9), in Nigeria ($346.4), and in China ($224.5). The growth of agriculture in Andorra was greater than in China (4.0%), in the USA (3.6%), in India (2.0%), and in Japan (-1.3%); but less than in Nigeria (10.1%).

The 2010s

The Andorra's agriculture was $17.0 million per year in the 2010s, ranked 195th in the world. The share in the world was 0.0005%, and 0.0047% in Europe.

The share of agriculture in the economy of Andorra was 0.60% in the 2010s, ranked 194th in the world.

The value added of agriculture per capita in Andorra was $213.5 in the 2010s, ranked 157th in the world, and was on a par with Ethiopia ($213.5), El Salvador ($213.2), Liechtenstein ($208.8). The Andorran agriculture per capita was less than agriculture per capita in the world ($432.1) in 2.0 times, and was less than agriculture per capita in Europe ($491.7) in 2.3 times.

The growth of agriculture in Andorra was 2.7% in the 2010s, ranked 79th in the world, and was on a par with Albania (2.7%). The growth of agriculture in Andorra (2.7%) was less than growth of agriculture in the world (2.9%), was greater than growth of agriculture in Europe (0.73%).

Comparison with neighbors. The sector of agriculture in Andorra was 2 484.6 times lower than in France ($42.3 billion) and 2 065.8 times lower than in Spain ($35.2 billion). The Andorra's agriculture per capita was 3.5 times lower than in Spain ($751.0) and 3.0 times lower than in France ($637.6). The growth of agriculture in Andorra was greater than in Spain (2.0%) and in France (0.17%).

Comparison with leaders. The Andorran agriculture was 52 068.6 times lower than in China ($886.2 billion), 21 351.6 times lower than in India ($363.4 billion), 10 592.6 times lower than in the United States ($180.3 billion), 7 288.3 times lower than in Indonesia ($124.1 billion), and 5 626.6 times lower than in Nigeria ($95.8 billion). The value of agriculture per capita in Andorra was 3.0 times lower than in China ($631.9), 2.6 times lower than in the USA ($564.3), 2.5 times lower than in Nigeria ($534.6), 2.3 times lower than in Indonesia ($483.6), and 23.5% lower than in India ($279.1). The growth of agriculture in Andorra was greater than in the United States (2.0%); but less than in India (4.1%), in Indonesia (3.9%), in China (3.8%), and in Nigeria (3.6%).

Chapter V. Industry

Mining, Manufacturing, Utilities (ISIC C-E)

The industry of Andorra enlarged from $14.2 million per year in the 1970s to $152.7 million per year in the 2010s, that is by $138.5 million or 10.7 times. The change occurred at $121.0 million due to a 4.8-fold increase in prices, as also at -$6.3 million due to a 1.2-fold decrease in productivity, as well as at $23.8 million due to the growing in population. The average annual growth in industry is 2.3%. The minimum value of industry was in 1970 at $5.5 million. The maximum value of industry was in 2008 at $186.8 million.

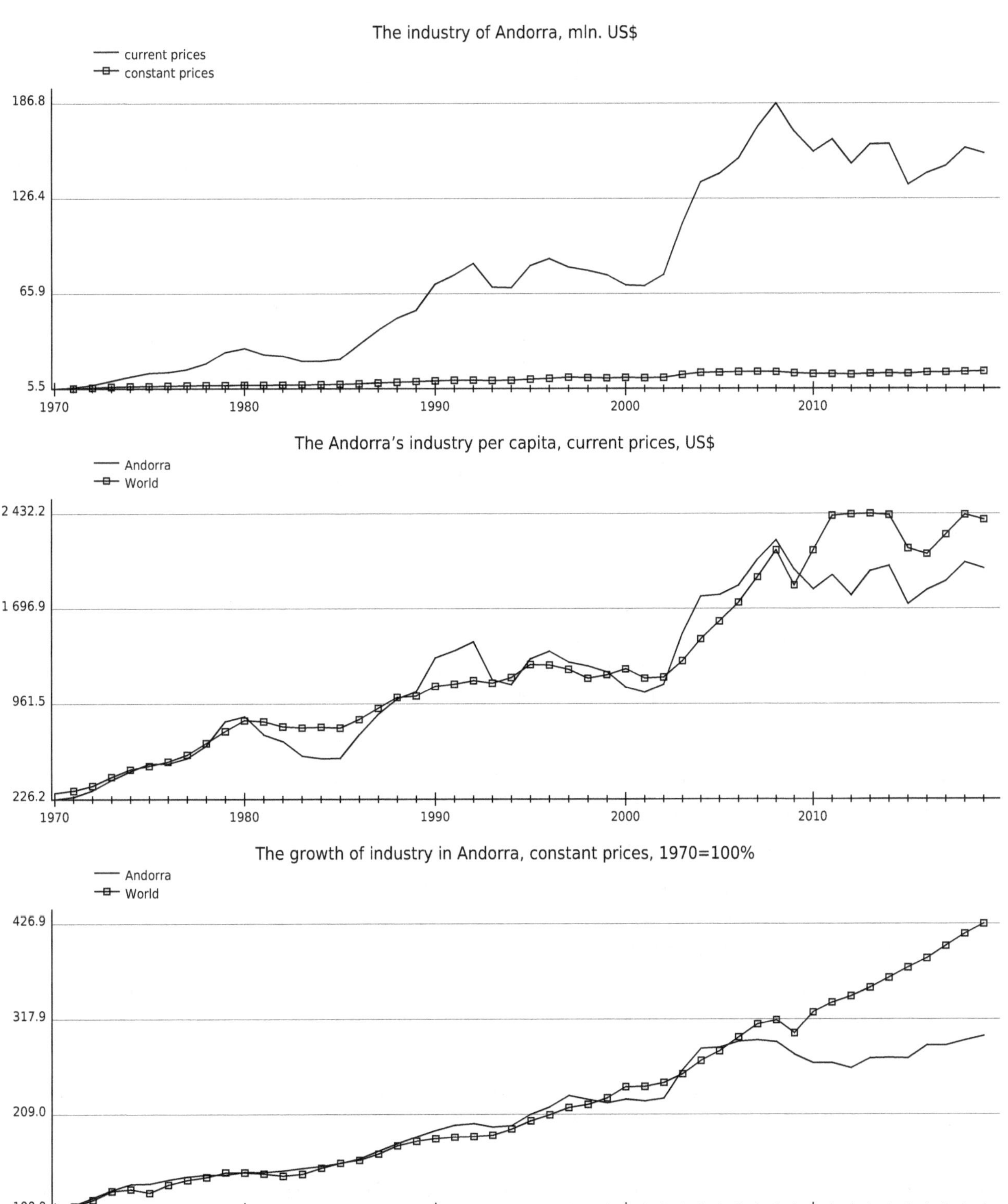

The industry of Andorra, mln. US$

The Andorra's industry per capita, current prices, US$

The growth of industry in Andorra, constant prices, 1970=100%

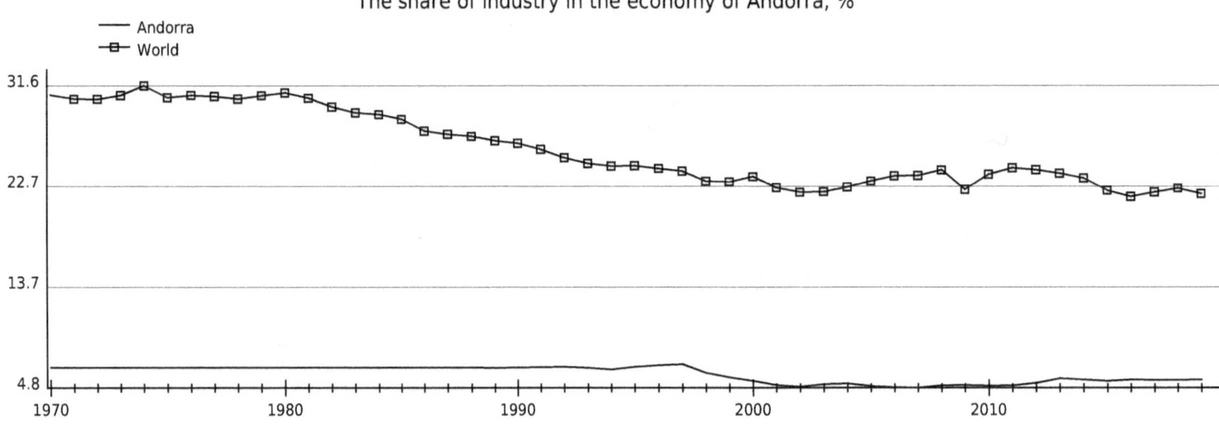

The 1970s

The Andorra's industry was $14.2 million per year in the 1970s, ranked 156th in the world. The share in the world was 0.0007%, and 0.0017% in Europe.

The share of industry in the economy of Andorra was 6.6% in the 1970s, ranked 163rd in the world, and was on a par with Dominica (6.6%), Gambia (6.6%).

The value added of industry per capita in Andorra was $477.6 in the 1970s, ranked 53rd in the world, and was on a par with the World ($480.5), Greenland ($480.5), South Africa ($469.8). The sector of industry per capita in Andorra was less than industry per capita in the world ($480.5) by 0.59%, and was less than industry per capita in Europe ($1 131.6) in 2.4 times.

The growth of industry in Andorra was 3.8% in the 1970s, ranked 115th in the world. The growth of industry in Andorra (3.8%) was less than growth of industry in the world (4.0%), was greater than growth of industry in Europe (3.6%).

Comparison with neighbors. The sector of industry in Andorra was less than in France ($71.6 billion) and in Spain ($29.8 billion). The value of industry per capita in Andorra was less than in France ($1 335.3) and in Spain ($836.9). The growth of industry in Andorra was less than in Spain (5.1%) and in France (3.9%).

Comparison with leaders. The value of industry in Andorra was less than in the United States ($450.4 billion), in the USSR ($248.8 billion), in Japan ($185.6 billion), in Germany ($158.4 billion), and in the UK ($72.6 billion). The value added of industry per capita in Andorra was less than in the USA ($2.1 thousand), in Germany ($2.0 thousand), in Japan ($1 666.5), in the United Kingdom ($1 295.1), and in the USSR ($986.6). The growth of industry in Andorra was greater than in the United States (2.4%), in Germany (2.1%), and in the UK (1.9%); but less than in the USSR (5.2%) and in Japan (4.5%).

The 1980s

The industry of Andorra was $33.7 million per year in the 1980s, ranked 155th in the world, and was on a par with Somalia ($34.4 million). The share in the world was 0.0008%, and 0.0023% in Europe.

The share of industry in the economy of Andorra was 6.6% in the 1980s, ranked 166th in the world.

The value of industry per capita in Andorra was $768.1 in the 1980s, ranked 62nd in the world, and was on a par with Bulgaria ($766.7), Hungary ($761.4), Portugal ($755.5). The sector of industry per capita in Andorra was less than industry per capita in the world ($861.8) by 10.9%, and was less than industry per capita in Europe ($1 933.8) in 2.5 times.

The growth of industry in Andorra was 2.7% in the 1980s, ranked 96th in the world, and was on a par with Middle Africa (2.7%). The growth of industry in Andorra (2.7%) was greater than growth of industry in the world (2.3%), was greater than growth of industry in Europe (2.3%).

Comparison with neighbors. The value of industry in Andorra was less than in France ($145.2 billion) and in Spain ($62.9 billion). The sector of industry per capita in Andorra was less than in France ($2.6 thousand) and in Spain ($1 630.8). The growth of industry in Andorra was greater than in Spain (2.0%) and in France (1.3%).

Comparison with leaders. The Andorran industry was less than in the USA ($1.0 trillion), in Japan ($566.4 billion), in the USSR ($305.7 billion), in Germany ($297.5 billion), and in the UK ($171.2 billion). The Andorran industry per capita was less than in Japan ($4.7

thousand), in the United States ($4.2 thousand), in Germany ($3.8 thousand), in the United Kingdom ($3.0 thousand), and in the USSR ($1 110.8). The growth of industry in Andorra was greater than in the USA (1.9%), in the United Kingdom (1.4%), and in Germany (1.2%); but less than in the USSR (5.3%) and in Japan (4.2%).

The 1990s

The sector of industry in Andorra was $78.6 million per year in the 1990s, ranked 174th in the world. The share in the world was 0.0012%, and 0.0037% in Europe.

The share of industry in the economy of Andorra was 6.5% in the 1990s, ranked 193rd in the world, and was on a par with Ethiopia (6.5%).

The industry per capita in Andorra was $1 279.2 in the 1990s, ranked 56th in the world, and was on a par with Venezuela ($1 277.0), Western Asia ($1 262.7). The sector of industry per capita in Andorra was greater than industry per capita in the world ($1 175.6) by 8.8%, and was less than industry per capita in Europe ($2 961.4) in 2.3 times.

The growth of industry in Andorra was 1.9% in the 1990s, ranked 122nd in the world, and was on a par with Malawi (1.9%), Algeria (1.9%), Poland (1.9%). The growth of industry in Andorra (1.9%) was less than growth of industry in the world (2.5%), was greater than growth of industry in Europe (0.0047%).

Comparison with neighbors. The industry of Andorra was less than in France ($253.9 billion) and in Spain ($119.2 billion). The Andorran industry per capita was less than in France ($4.3 thousand) and in Spain ($3.0 thousand). The growth of industry in Andorra was less than in France (2.4%) and in Spain (2.3%).

Comparison with leaders. The sector of industry in Andorra was less than in the USA ($1.5 trillion), in Japan ($1.2 trillion), in Germany ($534.0 billion), in China ($285.9 billion), and in the United Kingdom ($268.6 billion). The Andorra's industry per capita was greater than in China ($231.9); but less than in Japan ($9.4 thousand), in Germany ($6.6 thousand), in the USA ($5.7 thousand), and in the United Kingdom ($4.6 thousand). The growth of industry in Andorra was greater than in Japan (1.3%), in the United Kingdom (1.2%), and in Germany (0.33%); but less than in China (13.1%) and in the United States (2.8%).

The 2000s

The sector of industry in Andorra was $128.8 million per year in the 2000s, ranked 175th in the world, and was on a par with the Cayman Islands ($129.7 million), Burundi ($130.9 million). The share in the world was 0.0013%, and 0.0044% in Europe.

The share of industry in the economy of Andorra was 5.0% in the 2000s, ranked 200th in the world.

The sector of industry per capita in Andorra was $1 688.4 in the 2000s, ranked 61st in the world, and was on a par with Botswana ($1 651.7), Central America ($1 650.2). The value of industry per capita in Andorra was greater than industry per capita in the world ($1 573.8) by 7.3%, and was less than industry per capita in Europe ($4 000.9) in 2.4 times.

The growth of industry in Andorra was 2.3% in the 2000s, ranked 107th in the world, and was on a par with Saint Lucia (2.2%), Uruguay (2.3%). The growth of industry in Andorra (2.3%) was less than growth of industry in the world (2.9%), was greater than growth of industry in Europe (0.63%).

Comparison with neighbors. The Andorra's industry was less than in France ($304.8 billion) and in Spain ($179.3 billion). The Andorra's industry per capita was less than in France ($4.9 thousand) and in Spain ($4.1 thousand). The growth of industry in Andorra was greater than in Spain (0.73%) and in France (0.47%).

Comparison with leaders. The industry of Andorra was less than in the United States ($2.1 trillion), in Japan ($1.1 trillion), in China ($1.1 trillion), in Germany ($629.4 billion), and in the UK ($345.1 billion). The value added of industry per capita in Andorra was greater than in China ($795.3); but less than in Japan ($8.8 thousand), in Germany ($7.7 thousand), in the United States ($7.1 thousand), and in the UK ($5.7 thousand). The growth of industry in Andorra was greater than in the USA (1.5%), in Germany (0.19%), in Japan (0.15%), and in the United Kingdom (-1.1%); but less than in China (11.1%).

The 2010s

The sector of industry in Andorra was $152.7 million per year in the 2010s, ranked 180th in the world, and was on a par with the Maldives ($151.3 million), Djibouti ($154.9 million), Liberia ($156.6 million). The share in the world was 0.0009%, and 0.0040% in Europe.

The share of industry in the economy of Andorra was 5.4% in the 2010s, ranked 197th in the world.

The industry per capita in Andorra was $1 916.1 in the 2010s, ranked 75th in the world, and was on a par with Central America ($1 921.1), Suriname ($1 909.7), South America ($1 904.7). The sector of industry per capita in Andorra was less than industry per capita in the world ($2 320.9) by 17.4%, and was less than industry per capita in Europe ($5 088.1) in 2.7 times.

The growth of industry in Andorra was 0.7% in the 2010s, ranked 167th in the world. The growth of industry in Andorra (0.73%) was less than growth of industry in the world (3.5%), was less than growth of industry in Europe (2.0%).

Comparison with neighbors. The value added of industry in Andorra was 2 192.3 times lower than in France ($334.8 billion) and 1 313.5 times lower than in Spain ($200.6 billion). The value added of industry per capita in Andorra was 2.6 times lower than in France ($5.0 thousand) and 2.2 times lower than in Spain ($4.3 thousand). The growth of industry in Andorra was less than in France (0.89%) and in Spain (0.76%).

Comparison with leaders. The Andorra's industry was 24 116.1 times lower than in China ($3.7 trillion), 17 951.3 times lower than in the United States ($2.7 trillion), 7 794.4 times lower than in Japan ($1.2 trillion), 5 499.8 times lower than in Germany ($840.0 billion), and 2 903.1 times lower than in India ($443.4 billion). The sector of industry per capita in Andorra was 5.6 times higher than in India ($340.6); but 5.4 times lower than in Germany ($10.3 thousand), 4.9 times lower than in Japan ($9.3 thousand), 4.5 times lower than in the United States ($8.6 thousand), and 27.0% lower than in China ($2.6 thousand). The growth of industry in Andorra was less than in China (7.5%), in India (6.5%), in Germany (3.2%), in Japan (2.6%), and in the USA (2.2%).

Chapter 5.1. Manufacturing

(ISIC D)

The value added of manufacturing in Andorra enlarged from $9.4 million per year in the 1970s to $117.9 million per year in the 2010s, that is by $108.4 million or 12.5 times. The change occurred at $93.4 million due to a 4.8-fold increase in prices, as also at -$761.3 thousand due to a 1.0-fold decrease in productivity, as well as at $15.8 million due to the growing in population. The average annual growth in manufacturing is 2.5%. The minimum value of manufacturing was in 1970 at $3.6 million. The maximum value of manufacturing was in 2008 at $146.1 million.

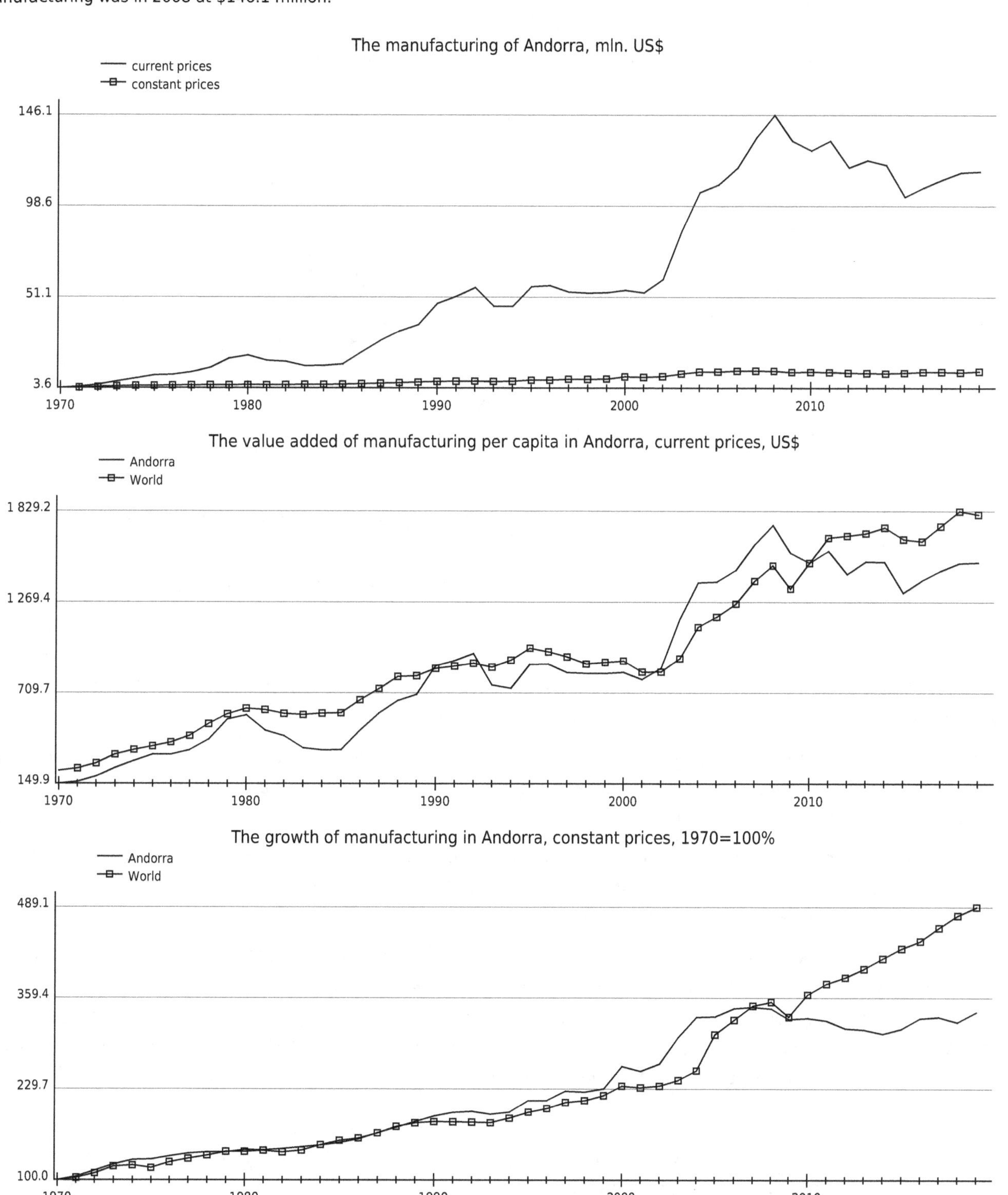

The manufacturing of Andorra, mln. US$

The value added of manufacturing per capita in Andorra, current prices, US$

The growth of manufacturing in Andorra, constant prices, 1970=100%

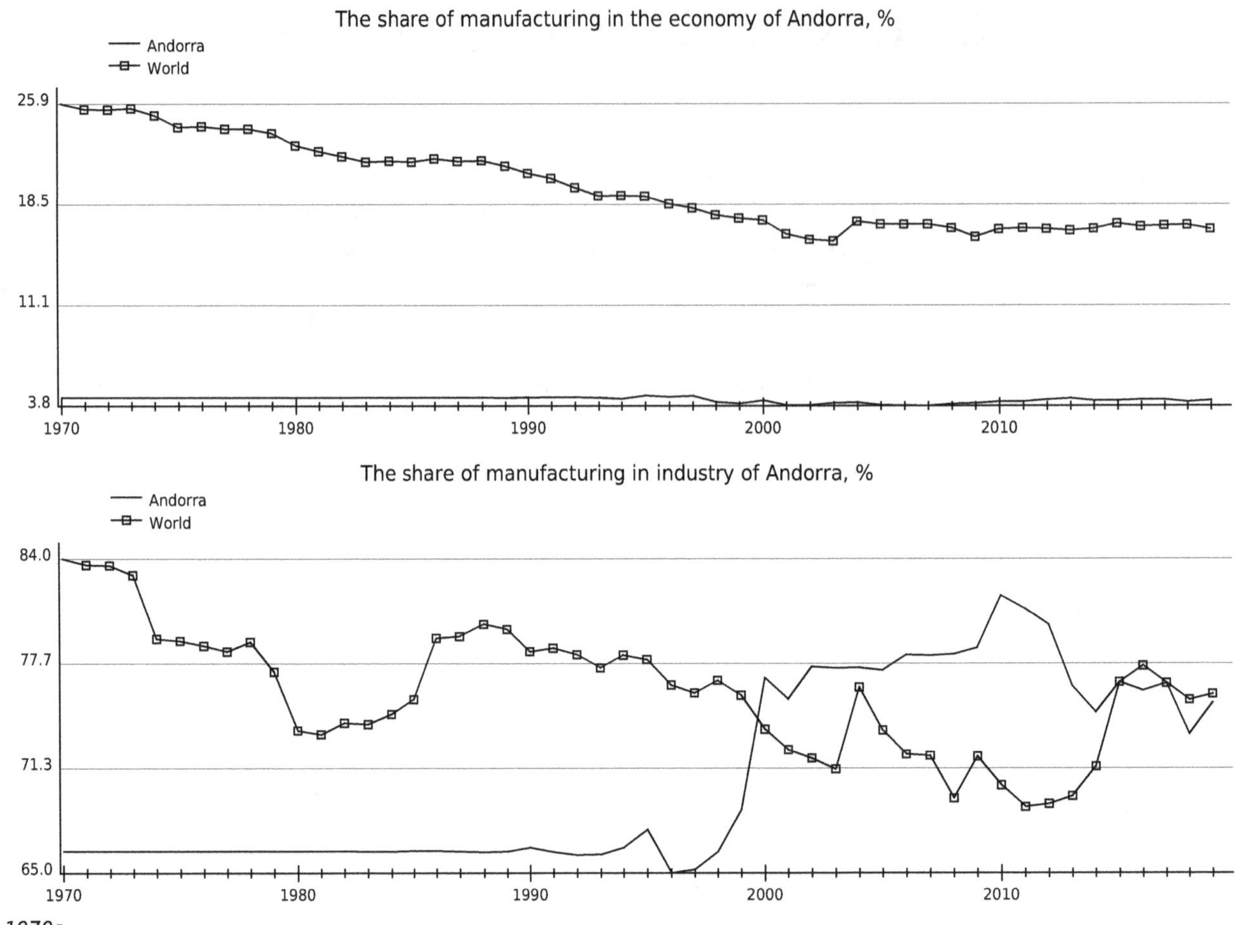

The share of manufacturing in the economy of Andorra, %

The share of manufacturing in industry of Andorra, %

The 1970s

The value added of manufacturing in Andorra was $9.4 million per year in the 1970s, ranked 152nd in the world. The share in the world was 0.0006%, and 0.0013% in Europe.

The share of manufacturing in the economy of Andorra was 4.4% in the 1970s, ranked 156th in the world, and was on a par with the Turks and Caicos Islands (4.4%).

The sector of manufacturing per capita in Andorra was $316.6 in the 1970s, ranked 50th in the world, and was on a par with French Polynesia ($320.4). The manufacturing per capita in Andorra was less than manufacturing per capita in the world ($383.2) by 17.4%, and was less than manufacturing per capita in Europe ($1 019.3) in 3.2 times.

The growth of manufacturing in Andorra was 3.8% in the 1970s, ranked 115th in the world, and was on a par with Jordan (3.8%), Anguilla (3.8%). The growth of manufacturing in Andorra (3.8%) was less than growth of manufacturing in the world (3.8%), was greater than growth of manufacturing in Europe (3.5%).

Comparison with neighbors. The value of manufacturing in Andorra was less than in France ($64.5 billion) and in Spain ($24.7 billion). The manufacturing per capita in Andorra was less than in France ($1 203.0) and in Spain ($692.0). The growth of manufacturing in Andorra was greater than in France (3.5%); but less than in Spain (5.1%).

Comparison with leaders. The value of manufacturing in Andorra was less than in the USA ($378.0 billion), in the USSR ($248.8 billion), in Japan ($169.3 billion), in Germany ($138.0 billion), and in France ($64.5 billion). The value added of manufacturing per capita in Andorra was less than in Germany ($1 752.1), in the United States ($1 731.8), in Japan ($1 520.6), in France ($1 203.0), and in the USSR ($986.6). The growth of manufacturing in Andorra was greater than in France (3.5%), in the United States (2.7%), and in Germany (2.1%); but less than in the USSR (5.2%) and in Japan (4.5%).

The 1980s

The Andorra's manufacturing was $22.3 million per year in the 1980s, ranked 152nd in the world, and was on a par with Laos ($21.9 million). The share in the world was 0.0007%, and 0.0017% in Europe.

The share of manufacturing in the economy of Andorra was 4.4% in the 1980s, ranked 163rd in the world, and was on a par with the Maldives (4.4%), Kiribati (4.4%), the TCI (4.4%).

The value of manufacturing per capita in Andorra was $509.0 in the 1980s, ranked 59th in the world, and was on a par with Central America ($509.0), Paraguay ($507.9), Bulgaria ($510.5). The value of manufacturing per capita in Andorra was less than manufacturing per capita in the world ($661.2) by 23.0%, and was less than manufacturing per capita in Europe ($1 672.2) in 3.3 times.

The growth of manufacturing in Andorra was 2.7% in the 1980s, ranked 98th in the world, and was on a par with Belgium (2.7%). The growth of manufacturing in Andorra (2.7%) was greater than growth of manufacturing in the world (2.6%), was greater than growth of manufacturing in Europe (2.1%).

Comparison with neighbors. The value added of manufacturing in Andorra was less than in France ($124.6 billion) and in Spain ($52.0 billion). The manufacturing per capita in Andorra was less than in France ($2.2 thousand) and in Spain ($1 348.4). The growth of manufacturing in Andorra was greater than in Spain (2.0%) and in France (1.0%).

Comparison with leaders. The value added of manufacturing in Andorra was less than in the USA ($789.4 billion), in Japan ($501.0 billion), in the USSR ($305.7 billion), in Germany ($258.7 billion), and in Italy ($134.1 billion). The value of manufacturing per capita in Andorra was less than in Japan ($4.1 thousand), in Germany ($3.3 thousand), in the United States ($3.3 thousand), in Italy ($2.4 thousand), and in the USSR ($1 110.8). The growth of manufacturing in Andorra was greater than in Italy (2.5%), in the United States (1.9%), and in Germany (1.2%); but less than in the USSR (5.3%) and in Japan (4.4%).

The 1990s

The manufacturing of Andorra was $52.2 million per year in the 1990s, ranked 170th in the world, and was on a par with Cape Verde ($51.0 million). The share in the world was 0.0010%, and 0.0029% in Europe.

The share of manufacturing in the economy of Andorra was 4.3% in the 1990s, ranked 185th in the world, and was on a par with Montserrat (4.3%).

The sector of manufacturing per capita in Andorra was $849.2 in the 1990s, ranked 52nd in the world, and was on a par with Eastern Asia ($851.3), Croatia ($852.3). The manufacturing per capita in Andorra was less than manufacturing per capita in the world ($908.4) by 6.5%, and was less than manufacturing per capita in Europe ($2 443.3) in 2.9 times.

The growth of manufacturing in Andorra was 2.3% in the 1990s, ranked 101st in the world, and was on a par with Portugal (2.3%), the Philippines (2.3%). The growth of manufacturing in Andorra (2.3%) was greater than growth of manufacturing in the world (2.0%), was greater than growth of manufacturing in Europe (0.24%).

Comparison with neighbors. The sector of manufacturing in Andorra was less than in France ($215.0 billion) and in Spain ($99.3 billion). The manufacturing per capita in Andorra was less than in France ($3.6 thousand) and in Spain ($2.5 thousand). The growth of manufacturing in Andorra was less than in Spain (2.5%) and in France (2.4%).

Comparison with leaders. The manufacturing of Andorra was less than in the USA ($1.2 trillion), in Japan ($1.0 trillion), in Germany ($468.8 billion), in Italy ($227.8 billion), and in France ($215.0 billion). The Andorra's manufacturing per capita was less than in Japan ($8.3 thousand), in Germany ($5.8 thousand), in the USA ($4.7 thousand), in Italy ($4.0 thousand), and in France ($3.6 thousand). The growth of manufacturing in Andorra was greater than in Italy (1.2%), in Japan (1.1%), and in Germany (0.26%); but less than in the United States (3.2%) and in France (2.4%).

The 2000s

The Andorran manufacturing was $100.2 million per year in the 2000s, ranked 171st in the world. The share in the world was 0.0014%, and 0.0043% in Europe.

The share of manufacturing in the economy of Andorra was 3.9% in the 2000s, ranked 187th in the world.

The manufacturing per capita in Andorra was $1 312.5 in the 2000s, ranked 51st in the world, and was on a par with Saudi Arabia ($1 309.0), Lithuania ($1 289.2), Poland ($1 281.9). The manufacturing per capita in Andorra was greater than manufacturing per capita in the world ($1 138.1) by 15.3%, and was less than manufacturing per capita in Europe ($3 162.1) in 2.4 times.

The growth of manufacturing in Andorra was 3.6% in the 2000s, ranked 85th in the world, and was on a par with Botswana (3.7%),

Micronesia (3.7%). The growth of manufacturing in Andorra (3.6%) was less than growth of manufacturing in the world (4.2%), was greater than growth of manufacturing in Europe (0.69%).

Comparison with neighbors. The sector of manufacturing in Andorra was less than in France ($256.2 billion) and in Spain ($148.2 billion). The value added of manufacturing per capita in Andorra was less than in France ($4.1 thousand) and in Spain ($3.4 thousand). The growth of manufacturing in Andorra was greater than in France (0.75%) and in Spain (0.021%).

Comparison with leaders. The Andorran manufacturing was less than in the USA ($1.6 trillion), in China ($1.1 trillion), in Japan ($992.9 billion), in Germany ($551.4 billion), and in Italy ($277.2 billion). The value of manufacturing per capita in Andorra was greater than in China ($815.3); but less than in Japan ($7.7 thousand), in Germany ($6.8 thousand), in the United States ($5.6 thousand), and in Italy ($4.8 thousand). The growth of manufacturing in Andorra was greater than in the USA (1.6%), in Japan (0.32%), in Germany (0.097%), and in Italy (-1.3%).

The 2010s

The value of manufacturing in Andorra was $117.9 million per year in the 2010s, ranked 175th in the world. The share in the world was 0.0009%, and 0.0041% in Europe.

The share of manufacturing in the economy of Andorra was 4.2% in the 2010s, ranked 181st in the world, and was on a par with Algeria (4.2%).

The value of manufacturing per capita in Andorra was $1 478.7 in the 2010s, ranked 64th in the world, and was on a par with Russia ($1 465.5), Belarus ($1 463.0). The value added of manufacturing per capita in Andorra was less than manufacturing per capita in the world ($1 697.4) by 12.9%, and was less than manufacturing per capita in Europe ($3 895.6) in 2.6 times.

The growth of manufacturing in Andorra was 0.3% in the 2010s, ranked 172nd in the world. The growth of manufacturing in Andorra (0.30%) was less than growth of manufacturing in the world (3.9%), was less than growth of manufacturing in Europe (2.5%).

Comparison with neighbors. The value of manufacturing in Andorra was 2 330.4 times lower than in France ($274.7 billion) and 1 291.7 times lower than in Spain ($152.2 billion). The value of manufacturing per capita in Andorra was 2.8 times lower than in France ($4.1 thousand) and 2.2 times lower than in Spain ($3.3 thousand). The growth of manufacturing in Andorra was less than in France (1.2%) and in Spain (0.66%).

Comparison with leaders. The value added of manufacturing in Andorra was 26 430.5 times lower than in China ($3.1 trillion), 17 567.6 times lower than in the United States ($2.1 trillion), 8 993.7 times lower than in Japan ($1.1 trillion), 6 237.8 times lower than in Germany ($735.2 billion), and 3 313.4 times lower than in Republic of Korea ($390.5 billion). The value added of manufacturing per capita in Andorra was 6.1 times lower than in Germany ($9.0 thousand), 5.6 times lower than in Japan ($8.3 thousand), 5.2 times lower than in South Korea ($7.7 thousand), 4.4 times lower than in the USA ($6.5 thousand), and 33.4% lower than in China ($2.2 thousand). The growth of manufacturing in Andorra was less than in China (7.5%), in South Korea (3.8%), in Germany (3.5%), in Japan (3.0%), and in the United States (1.9%).

Chapter VI. Construction

(ISIC F)

The Andorra's construction grew up from $25.2 million per year in the 1970s to $195.3 million per year in the 2010s, that is by $170.1 million or 7.7 times. The change occurred at $155.1 million due to a 4.9-fold increase in prices, as also at -$27.2 million due to a 1.7-fold decrease in productivity, as well as at $42.2 million due to the expansion in population. The average annual growth in construction is 1.3%. The minimum value of construction was in 1970 at $9.7 million. The maximum value of construction was in 2008 at $443.7 million.

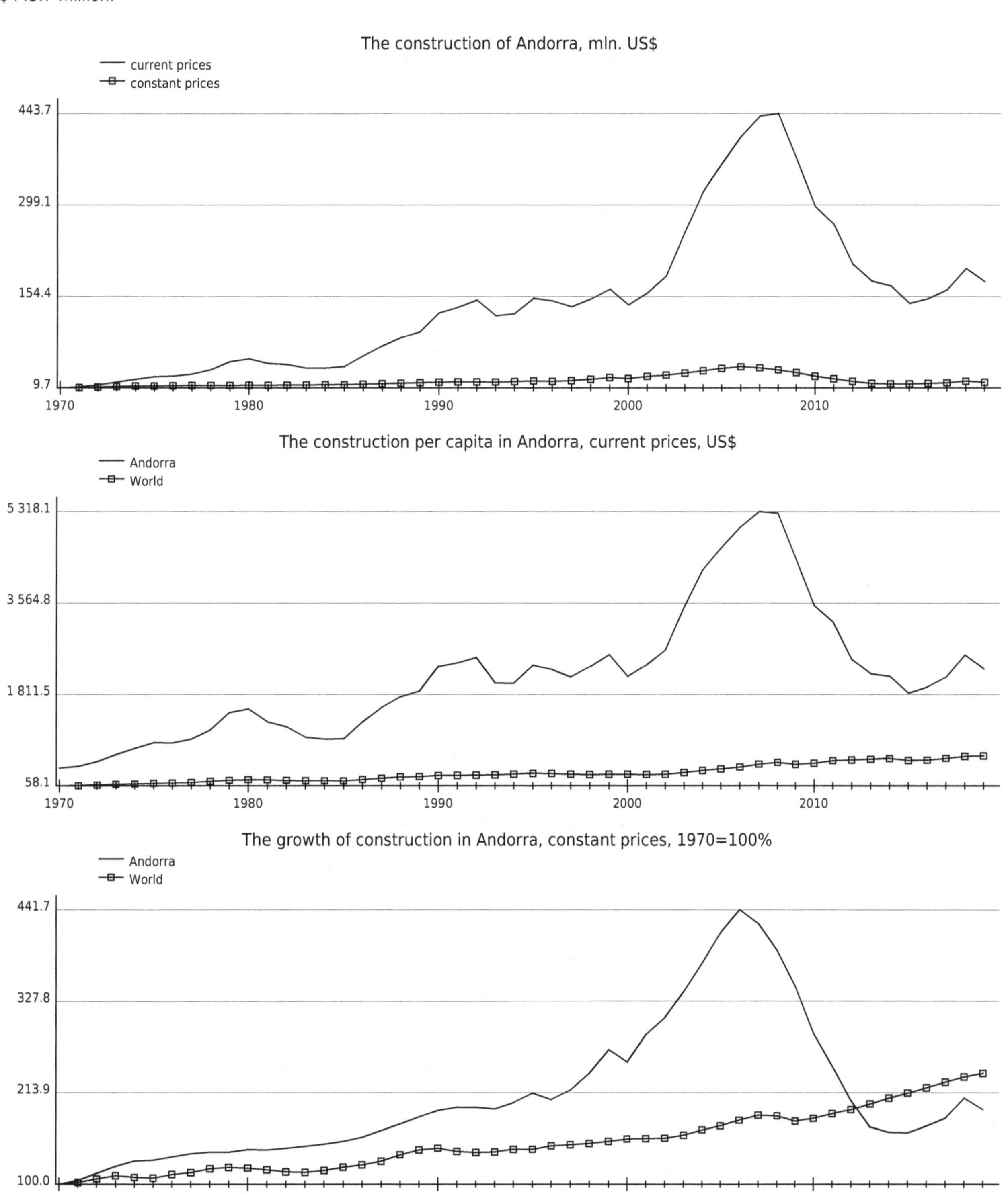

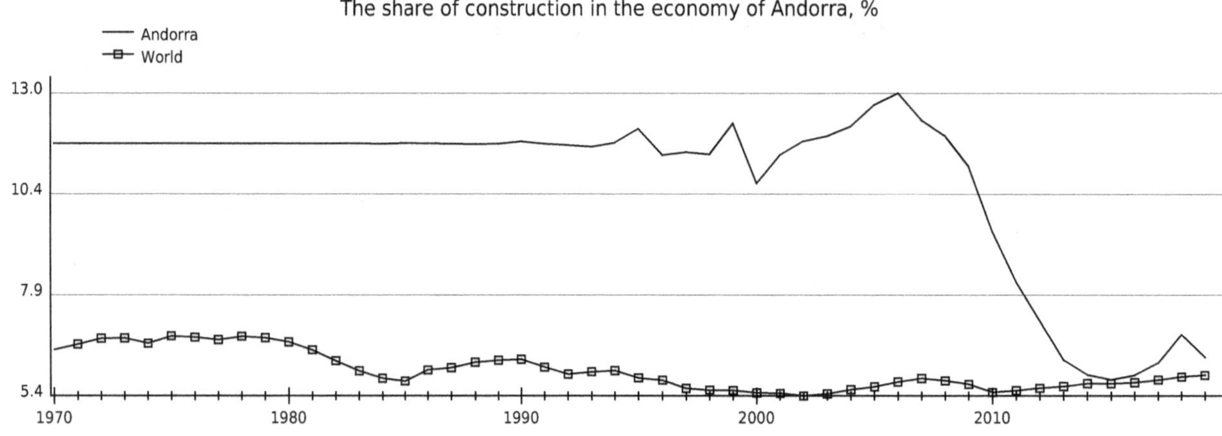

The 1970s

The value of construction in Andorra was $25.2 million per year in the 1970s, ranked 133rd in the world. The share in the world was 0.0059%, and 0.013% in Europe.

The share of construction in the economy of Andorra was 11.7% in the 1970s, ranked 12th in the world.

The Andorran construction per capita was $846.3 in the 1970s, ranked 6th in the world, and was on a par with Iceland ($865.7). The value of construction per capita in Andorra was greater than construction per capita in the world ($106.1) in 8.0 times, and was greater than construction per capita in Europe ($277.9) in 3.0 times.

The growth of construction in Andorra was 3.8% in the 1970s, ranked 102nd in the world, and was on a par with Anguilla (3.8%). The growth of construction in Andorra (3.8%) was greater than growth of construction in the world (2.1%), was greater than growth of construction in Europe (1.3%).

Comparison with neighbors. The value added of construction in Andorra was less than in France ($22.4 billion) and in Spain ($10.5 billion). The value added of construction per capita in Andorra was greater than in France ($417.3) and in Spain ($295.7). The growth of construction in Andorra was greater than in France (2.0%) and in Spain (0.19%).

Comparison with leaders. The Andorran construction was less than in the USA ($81.1 billion), in the USSR ($52.5 billion), in Japan ($43.5 billion), in Germany ($33.8 billion), and in France ($22.4 billion). The construction per capita in Andorra was greater than in Germany ($428.6), in France ($417.3), in Japan ($390.8), in the USA ($371.5), and in the USSR ($208.1). The growth of construction in Andorra was greater than in Japan (3.4%), in France (2.0%), in Germany (0.66%), and in the United States (0.31%); but less than in the USSR (6.5%).

The 1980s

The value of construction in Andorra was $59.7 million per year in the 1980s, ranked 135th in the world, and was on a par with Guyana ($60.1 million), Senegal ($61.1 million). The share in the world was 0.0066%, and 0.017% in Europe.

The share of construction in the economy of Andorra was 11.7% in the 1980s, ranked 11th in the world.

The construction per capita in Andorra was $1 361.0 in the 1980s, ranked 7th in the world. The Andorra's construction per capita was greater than construction per capita in the world ($186.2) in 7.3 times, and was greater than construction per capita in Europe ($462.7) in 2.9 times.

The growth of construction in Andorra was 2.8% in the 1980s, ranked 84th in the world, and was on a par with Ethiopia (2.8%). The growth of construction in Andorra (2.8%) was greater than growth of construction in the world (1.7%), was greater than growth of construction in Europe (1.9%).

Comparison with neighbors. The value of construction in Andorra was less than in France ($42.5 billion) and in Spain ($20.9 billion). The value of construction per capita in Andorra was greater than in France ($751.9) and in Spain ($543.1). The growth of construction in Andorra was greater than in Spain (2.6%) and in France (0.67%).

Comparison with leaders. The value of construction in Andorra was less than in the USA ($180.6 billion), in Japan ($138.7 billion), in the USSR ($72.1 billion), in Germany ($57.8 billion), and in France ($42.5 billion). The value of construction per capita in Andorra was greater than in Japan ($1 143.9), in the United States ($754.4), in France ($751.9), in Germany ($740.2), and in the USSR ($262.0). The growth of construction in Andorra was greater than in Japan (2.1%), in the USA (1.1%), in France (0.67%), and in Germany (-0.52%); but less than in the USSR (6.2%).

The 1990s

The value of construction in Andorra was $141.7 million per year in the 1990s, ranked 137th in the world, and was on a par with Bermuda ($141.9 million), Myanmar ($145.3 million). The share in the world was 0.0089%, and 0.026% in Europe.

The share of construction in the economy of Andorra was 11.7% in the 1990s, ranked 7th in the world.

The sector of construction per capita in Andorra was $2 305.3 in the 1990s, ranked 8th in the world. The Andorran construction per capita was greater than construction per capita in the world ($278.6) in 8.3 times, and was greater than construction per capita in Europe ($760.7) in 3.0 times.

The growth of construction in Andorra was 3.8% in the 1990s, ranked 80th in the world, and was on a par with Anguilla (3.8%), Eastern Africa (3.8%), South Korea (3.8%). The growth of construction in Andorra (3.8%) was greater than growth of construction in the world (0.71%), was greater than growth of construction in Europe (-1.7%).

Comparison with neighbors. The sector of construction in Andorra was less than in France ($68.8 billion) and in Spain ($52.1 billion). The value added of construction per capita in Andorra was greater than in Spain ($1 309.7) and in France ($1 158.8). The growth of construction in Andorra was greater than in Spain (1.5%) and in France (-0.65%).

Comparison with leaders. The Andorran construction was less than in Japan ($343.2 billion), in the United States ($299.1 billion), in Germany ($125.2 billion), in the United Kingdom ($69.8 billion), and in France ($68.8 billion). The sector of construction per capita in Andorra was greater than in Germany ($1 552.3), in the United Kingdom ($1 205.1), in France ($1 158.8), and in the United States ($1 131.2); but less than in Japan ($2.7 thousand). The growth of construction in Andorra was greater than in the USA (1.8%), in Germany (-0.047%), in the UK (-0.34%), in France (-0.65%), and in Japan (-1.0%).

The 2000s

The value of construction in Andorra was $309.2 million per year in the 2000s, ranked 133rd in the world, and was on a par with Nicaragua ($313.8 million), Georgia ($303.5 million). The share in the world was 0.012%, and 0.037% in Europe.

The share of construction in the economy of Andorra was 12.0% in the 2000s, ranked 8th in the world.

The value added of construction per capita in Andorra was $4 052.1 in the 2000s, ranked 5th in the world. The Andorran construction per capita was greater than construction per capita in the world ($381.3) in 10.6 times, and was greater than construction per capita in Europe ($1 147.4) in 3.5 times.

The growth of construction in Andorra was 2.6% in the 2000s, ranked 134th in the world, and was on a par with North Korea (2.6%), Botswana (2.7%), Luxembourg (2.7%). The growth of construction in Andorra (2.6%) was greater than growth of construction in the world (1.5%), was greater than growth of construction in Europe (0.97%).

Comparison with neighbors. The construction of Andorra was less than in Spain ($111.8 billion) and in France ($106.0 billion). The sector of construction per capita in Andorra was greater than in Spain ($2.6 thousand) and in France ($1 688.4). The growth of construction in Andorra was greater than in Spain (1.7%) and in France (1.3%).

Comparison with leaders. The sector of construction in Andorra was less than in the USA ($583.0 billion), in Japan ($270.5 billion), in China ($150.1 billion), in the UK ($132.1 billion), and in Spain ($111.8 billion). The value added of construction per capita in Andorra was greater than in Spain ($2.6 thousand), in the UK ($2.2 thousand), in Japan ($2.1 thousand), in the United States ($1 983.7), and in China ($113.1). The growth of construction in Andorra was greater than in Spain (1.7%), in the United Kingdom (0.17%), in the USA (-2.6%), and in Japan (-3.9%); but less than in China (11.9%).

The 2010s

The Andorra's construction was $195.3 million per year in the 2010s, ranked 167th in the world, and was on a par with French Polynesia ($195.9 million). The share in the world was 0.0047%, and 0.019% in Europe.

The share of construction in the economy of Andorra was 6.9% in the 2010s, ranked 74th in the world, and was on a par with Finland (6.8%), Western Asia (6.8%).

The value of construction per capita in Andorra was $2 450.5 in the 2010s, ranked 21st in the world, and was on a par with Northern Europe ($2.4 thousand). The value added of construction per capita in Andorra was greater than construction per capita in the world ($572.1) in 4.3 times, and was greater than construction per capita in Europe ($1 415.6) by 73.1%.

The growth of construction in Andorra was -5.7% in the 2010s, ranked 197th in the world. The growth of construction in Andorra (-5.7%) was less than growth of construction in the world (2.9%), was less than growth of construction in Europe (0.50%).

Comparison with neighbors. The Andorra's construction was 706.2 times lower than in France ($137.9 billion) and 409.2 times lower than in Spain ($79.9 billion). The value of construction per capita in Andorra was 17.8% higher than in France ($2.1 thousand) and 43.5% higher than in Spain ($1 707.2). The growth of construction in Andorra was less than in France (-0.78%) and in Spain (-3.3%).

Comparison with leaders. The Andorra's construction was 3 743.0 times lower than in China ($731.1 billion), 3 485.5 times lower than in the USA ($680.8 billion), 1 426.7 times lower than in Japan ($278.7 billion), 860.6 times lower than in India ($168.1 billion), and 784.5 times lower than in Germany ($153.2 billion). The sector of construction per capita in Andorra was 12.5% higher than in Japan ($2.2 thousand), 15.0% higher than in the USA ($2.1 thousand), 30.9% higher than in Germany ($1 871.9), 4.7 times higher than in China ($521.3), and 19.0 times higher than in India ($129.1). The growth of construction in Andorra was less than in China (8.2%), in India (5.2%), in Germany (1.8%), in Japan (1.7%), and in the USA (1.4%).

Chapter VII. Transportation

Transport, storage and communication (ISIC I)

The Andorra's transportation increased from $8.0 million per year in the 1970s to $158.9 million per year in the 2010s, that is by $151.0 million or 20.0 times. The change occurred at $125.8 million due to a 4.8-fold increase in prices, as also at $11.9 million due to a 1.6-fold increase in productivity, as well as at $13.3 million due to the increase in population. The average annual growth in transportation is 3.7%. The minimum value of transportation was in 1970 at $3.1 million. The maximum value of transportation was in 2008 at $187.1 million.

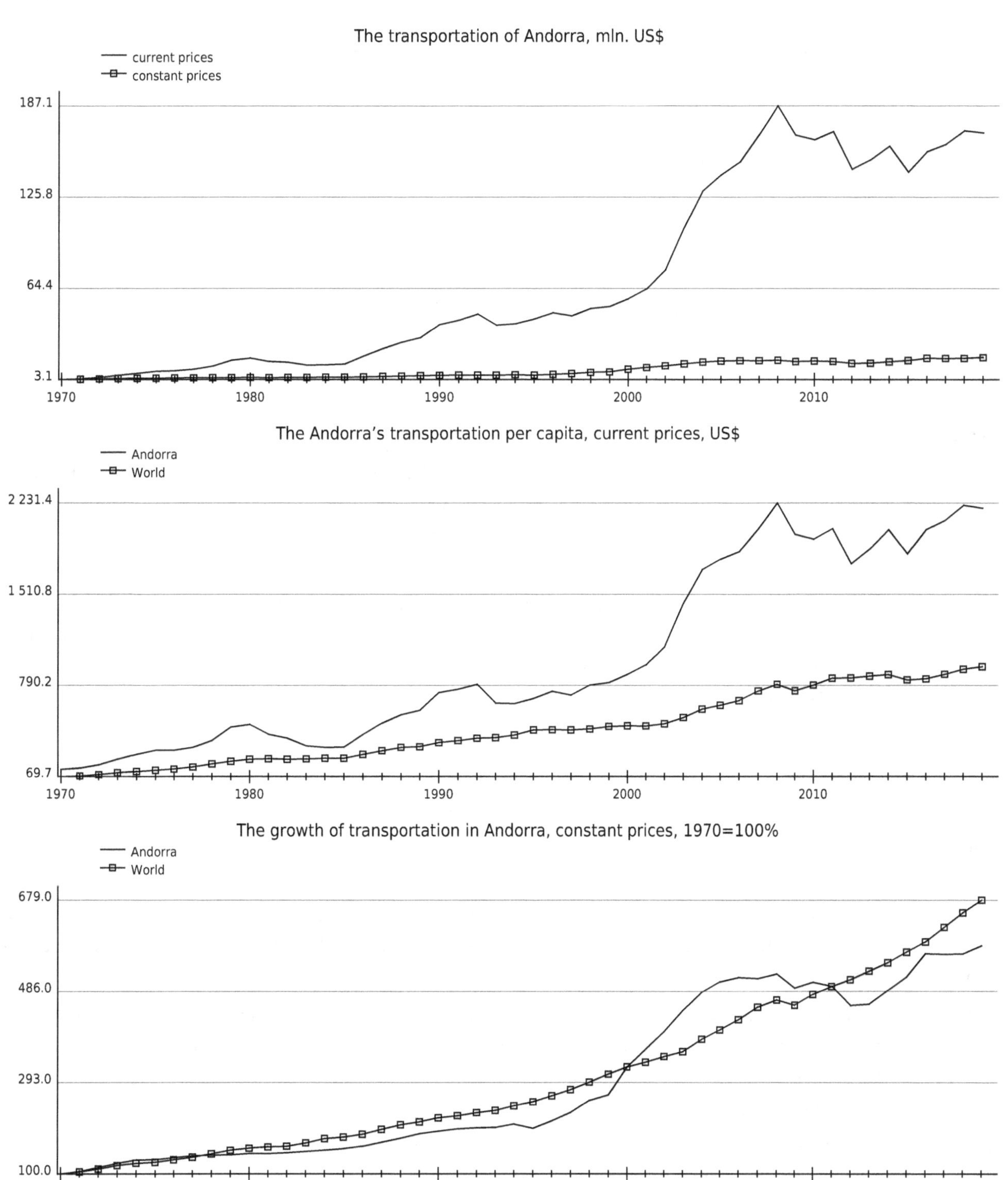

The transportation of Andorra, mln. US$

The Andorra's transportation per capita, current prices, US$

The growth of transportation in Andorra, constant prices, 1970=100%

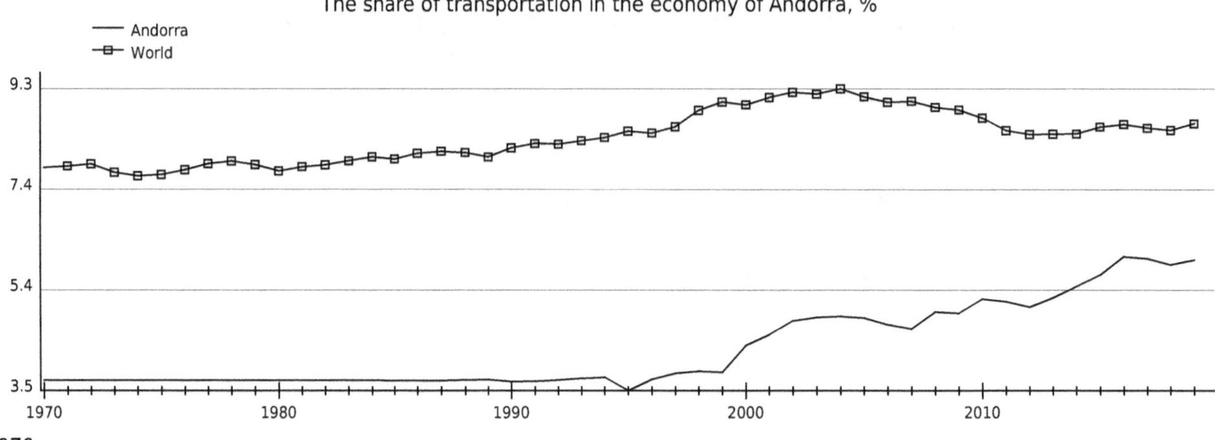

The share of transportation in the economy of Andorra, %

The 1970s

The Andorran transportation was $8.0 million per year in the 1970s, ranked 151st in the world, and was on a par with Samoa ($7.9 million). The share in the world was 0.0016%, and 0.0044% in Europe.

The share of transportation in the economy of Andorra was 3.7% in the 1970s, ranked 159th in the world, and was on a par with Palestine (3.7%), New Caledonia (3.7%).

The value added of transportation per capita in Andorra was $266.7 in the 1970s, ranked 36th in the world, and was on a par with Bahrain ($265.2). The sector of transportation per capita in Andorra was greater than transportation per capita in the world ($122.3) in 2.2 times, and was greater than transportation per capita in Europe ($248.3) by 7.4%.

The growth of transportation in Andorra was 3.8% in the 1970s, ranked 129th in the world, and was on a par with Saint Vincent and the Grenadines (3.8%). The growth of transportation in Andorra (3.8%) was less than growth of transportation in the world (4.6%), was less than growth of transportation in Europe (4.3%).

Comparison with neighbors. The value of transportation in Andorra was less than in France ($24.0 billion) and in Spain ($7.6 billion). The value added of transportation per capita in Andorra was greater than in Spain ($213.7); but less than in France ($447.4). The growth of transportation in Andorra was less than in Spain (4.6%) and in France (4.1%).

Comparison with leaders. The transportation of Andorra was less than in the USA ($168.6 billion), in Japan ($46.4 billion), in Germany ($29.6 billion), in the USSR ($28.8 billion), and in France ($24.0 billion). The value of transportation per capita in Andorra was greater than in the USSR ($114.0); but less than in the USA ($772.4), in France ($447.4), in Japan ($416.6), and in Germany ($376.1). The growth of transportation in Andorra was greater than in Germany (3.0%) and in Japan (1.7%); but less than in the USSR (8.1%), in the USA (4.2%), and in France (4.1%).

The 1980s

The transportation of Andorra was $18.8 million per year in the 1980s, ranked 153rd in the world, and was on a par with Micronesia ($18.6 million). The share in the world was 0.0016%, and 0.0050% in Europe.

The share of transportation in the economy of Andorra was 3.7% in the 1980s, ranked 163rd in the world, and was on a par with Guinea-Bissau (3.7%), Palestine (3.7%).

The Andorra's transportation per capita was $429.3 in the 1980s, ranked 43rd in the world, and was on a par with Polynesia ($434.5). The value of transportation per capita in Andorra was greater than transportation per capita in the world ($242.0) by 77.4%, and was less than transportation per capita in Europe ($494.5) by 13.2%.

The growth of transportation in Andorra was 2.8% in the 1980s, ranked 122nd in the world, and was on a par with Uganda (2.8%). The growth of transportation in Andorra (2.8%) was less than growth of transportation in the world (3.4%), was greater than growth of transportation in Europe (2.8%).

Comparison with neighbors. The sector of transportation in Andorra was less than in France ($56.2 billion) and in Spain ($20.1 billion). The value of transportation per capita in Andorra was less than in France ($993.7) and in Spain ($520.9). The growth of transportation in Andorra was greater than in Spain (1.9%); but less than in France (5.4%).

Comparison with leaders. The value added of transportation in Andorra was less than in the USA ($394.9 billion), in Japan ($147.7 billion), in Germany ($56.6 billion), in France ($56.2 billion), and in the United Kingdom ($53.0 billion). The transportation per capita in Andorra was less than in the United States ($1 649.2), in Japan ($1 217.8), in France ($993.7), in the United Kingdom ($938.7), and in Germany ($725.5). The growth of transportation in Andorra was greater than in Germany (1.8%); but less than in France (5.4%), in Japan (4.7%), in the USA (3.6%), and in the UK (3.0%).

The 1990s

The sector of transportation in Andorra was $45.1 million per year in the 1990s, ranked 177th in the world. The share in the world was 0.0019%, and 0.0057% in Europe.

The share of transportation in the economy of Andorra was 3.7% in the 1990s, ranked 194th in the world, and was on a par with Laos (3.8%), Malawi (3.7%), Botswana (3.7%).

The sector of transportation per capita in Andorra was $733.6 in the 1990s, ranked 46th in the world. The value of transportation per capita in Andorra was greater than transportation per capita in the world ($409.5) by 79.1%, and was less than transportation per capita in Europe ($1 080.1) by 32.1%.

The growth of transportation in Andorra was 3.8% in the 1990s, ranked 118th in the world, and was on a par with Djibouti (3.7%), Western Europe (3.8%), Austria (3.8%). The growth of transportation in Andorra (3.8%) was less than growth of transportation in the world (4.0%), was greater than growth of transportation in Europe (2.4%).

Comparison with neighbors. The value of transportation in Andorra was less than in France ($118.7 billion) and in Spain ($49.2 billion). The sector of transportation per capita in Andorra was less than in France ($1 999.2) and in Spain ($1 238.8). The growth of transportation in Andorra was greater than in Spain (2.1%); but less than in France (4.8%).

Comparison with leaders. The transportation of Andorra was less than in the United States ($702.6 billion), in Japan ($373.9 billion), in Germany ($144.3 billion), in France ($118.7 billion), and in the UK ($117.6 billion). The sector of transportation per capita in Andorra was less than in Japan ($3.0 thousand), in the USA ($2.7 thousand), in the United Kingdom ($2.0 thousand), in France ($1 999.2), and in Germany ($1 789.0). The growth of transportation in Andorra was greater than in Japan (3.0%); but less than in the United States (5.0%), in France (4.8%), in the UK (4.7%), and in Germany (3.9%).

The 2000s

The Andorra's transportation was $124.7 million per year in the 2000s, ranked 171st in the world, and was on a par with Antigua and Barbuda ($124.9 million), Swaziland ($123.4 million), Laos ($126.4 million). The share in the world was 0.0031%, and 0.0092% in Europe.

The share of transportation in the economy of Andorra was 4.8% in the 2000s, ranked 187th in the world.

The transportation per capita in Andorra was $1 633.7 in the 2000s, ranked 44th in the world, and was on a par with Malta ($1 628.0). The value of transportation per capita in Andorra was greater than transportation per capita in the world ($621.1) in 2.6 times, and was less than transportation per capita in Europe ($1 850.1) by 11.7%.

The growth of transportation in Andorra was 6.3% in the 2000s, ranked 79th in the world, and was on a par with Ireland (6.3%), Anguilla (6.3%), Malawi (6.3%). The growth of transportation in Andorra (6.3%) was greater than growth of transportation in the world (3.9%), was greater than growth of transportation in Europe (3.1%).

Comparison with neighbors. The Andorra's transportation was less than in France ($185.6 billion) and in Spain ($85.8 billion). The sector of transportation per capita in Andorra was less than in France ($3.0 thousand) and in Spain ($1 963.8). The growth of transportation in Andorra was greater than in France (2.7%) and in Spain (2.1%).

Comparison with leaders. The sector of transportation in Andorra was less than in the USA ($1.2 trillion), in Japan ($468.5 billion), in Germany ($228.2 billion), in the UK ($215.9 billion), and in France ($185.6 billion). The sector of transportation per capita in Andorra was less than in the USA ($4.0 thousand), in Japan ($3.7 thousand), in the United Kingdom ($3.6 thousand), in France ($3.0 thousand), and in Germany ($2.8 thousand). The growth of transportation in Andorra was greater than in Germany (3.4%), in the UK (3.1%), in the United States (3.1%), in France (2.7%), and in Japan (1.5%).

The 2010s

The sector of transportation in Andorra was $158.9 million per year in the 2010s, ranked 176th in the world, and was on a par with Sierra Leone ($156.6 million), Saint Lucia ($162.1 million). The share in the world was 0.0025%, and 0.0088% in Europe.

The share of transportation in the economy of Andorra was 5.6% in the 2010s, ranked 179th in the world, and was on a par with the Solomon Islands (5.6%), Nicaragua (5.6%), Liberia (5.6%).

The value of transportation per capita in Andorra was $1 994.0 in the 2010s, ranked 52nd in the world, and was on a par with the Cook Islands ($2.0 thousand). The value of transportation per capita in Andorra was greater than transportation per capita in the world ($864.8) in 2.3 times, and was less than transportation per capita in Europe ($2 422.4) by 17.7%.

The growth of transportation in Andorra was 1.7% in the 2010s, ranked 173rd in the world. The growth of transportation in Andorra (1.7%) was less than growth of transportation in the world (4.0%), was less than growth of transportation in Europe (2.6%).

Comparison with neighbors. The Andorra's transportation was 1 459.9 times lower than in France ($232.0 billion) and 652.6 times lower than in Spain ($103.7 billion). The Andorran transportation per capita was 43.0% lower than in France ($3.5 thousand) and 10.0% lower than in Spain ($2.2 thousand). The growth of transportation in Andorra was less than in Spain (2.7%) and in France (2.6%).

Comparison with leaders. The value of transportation in Andorra was 11 252.3 times lower than in the United States ($1.8 trillion), 3 333.5 times lower than in Japan ($529.8 billion), 2 920.9 times lower than in China ($464.2 billion), 1 887.7 times lower than in Germany ($300.0 billion), and 1 621.7 times lower than in the UK ($257.7 billion). The Andorra's transportation per capita was 6.0 times higher than in China ($331.0); but 2.8 times lower than in the USA ($5.6 thousand), 2.1 times lower than in Japan ($4.1 thousand), 49.3% lower than in the UK ($3.9 thousand), and 45.6% lower than in Germany ($3.7 thousand). The growth of transportation in Andorra was greater than in Japan (0.81%); but less than in China (7.5%), in the USA (5.1%), in the UK (2.8%), and in Germany (2.7%).

Chapter VIII. Trade

Wholesale, retail trade, restaurants and hotels (ISIC G-H)

The value added of trade in Andorra increased from $87.3 million per year in the 1970s to $712.5 million per year in the 2010s, that is by $625.2 million or 8.2 times. The change occurred at $564.7 million due to a 4.8-fold increase in prices, as also at -$85.5 million due to a 1.6-fold decrease in productivity, as well as at $146.0 million due to the increase in population. The average annual growth in trade is 1.6%. The minimum value of trade was in 1970 at $33.7 million. The maximum value of trade was in 2008 at $974.8 million.

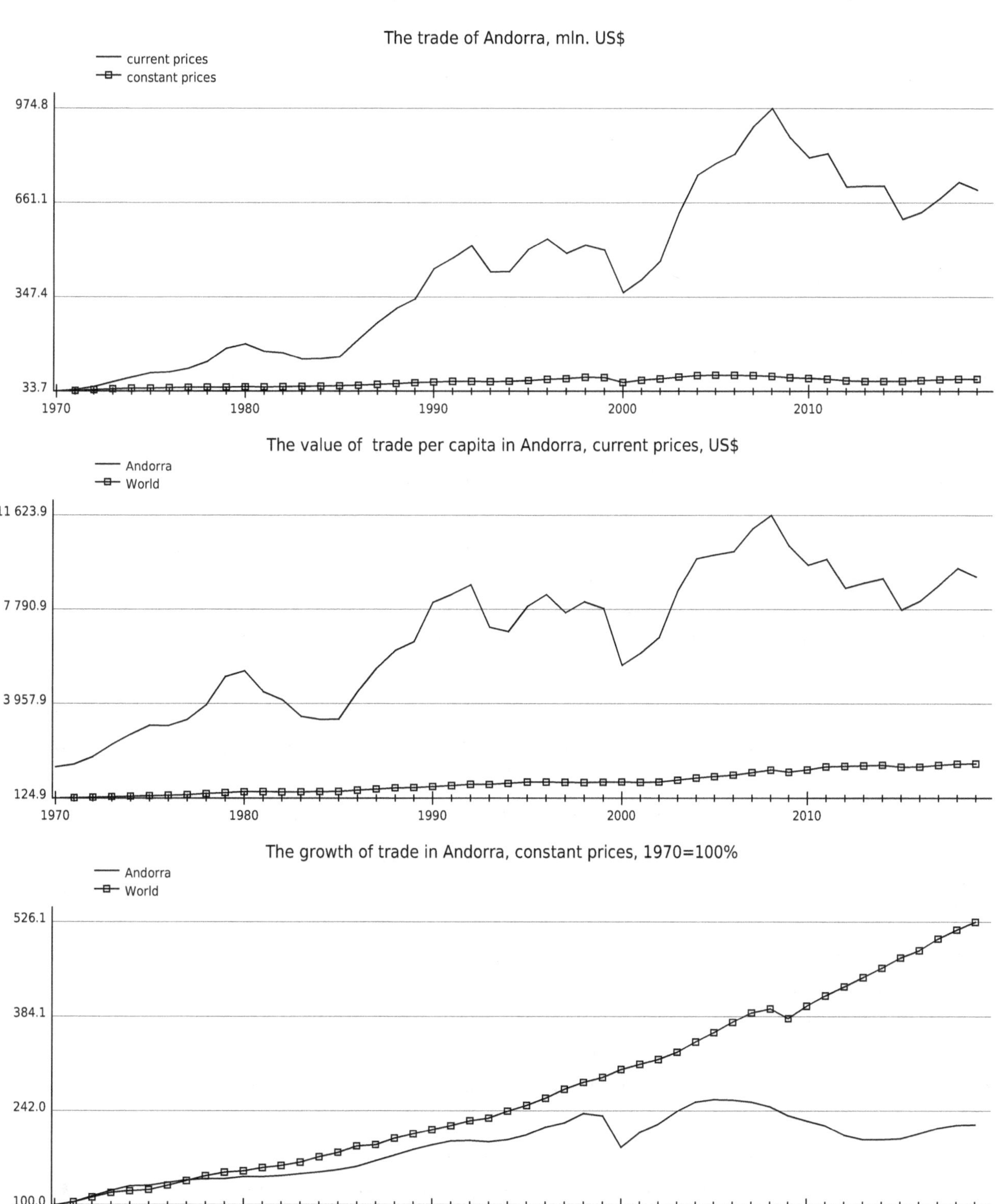

The trade of Andorra, mln. US$

The value of trade per capita in Andorra, current prices, US$

The growth of trade in Andorra, constant prices, 1970=100%

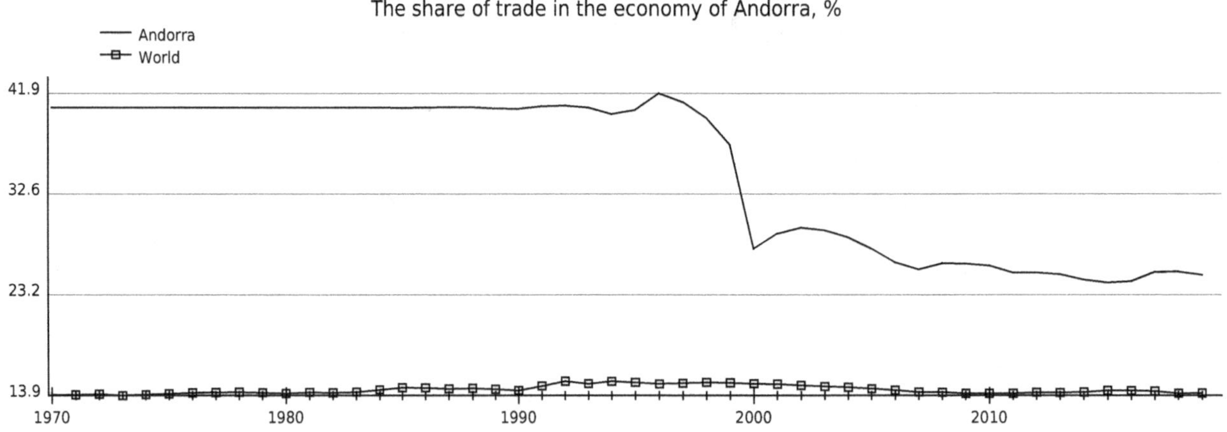

The 1970s

The value added of trade in Andorra was $87.3 million per year in the 1970s, ranked 127th in the world, and was on a par with Aruba ($86.3 million), Namibia ($89.4 million). The share in the world was 0.0098%, and 0.027% in Europe.

The share of trade in the economy of Andorra was 40.6% in the 1970s, ranked 1st in the world.

The trade per capita in Andorra was $2 927.3 in the 1970s, ranked 3rd in the world. The Andorra's trade per capita was greater than trade per capita in the world ($221.0) in 13.2 times, and was greater than trade per capita in Europe ($450.1) in 6.5 times.

The growth of trade in Andorra was 3.8% in the 1970s, ranked 115th in the world, and was on a par with Bhutan (3.8%), Italy (3.8%). The growth of trade in Andorra (3.8%) was less than growth of trade in the world (4.5%), was greater than growth of trade in Europe (3.6%).

Comparison with neighbors. The Andorran trade was less than in France ($40.9 billion) and in Spain ($16.3 billion). The Andorra's trade per capita was greater than in France ($762.4) and in Spain ($456.1). The growth of trade in Andorra was less than in Spain (4.6%) and in France (3.9%).

Comparison with leaders. The sector of trade in Andorra was less than in the United States ($278.3 billion), in Japan ($90.3 billion), in the USSR ($62.3 billion), in Germany ($61.1 billion), and in France ($40.9 billion). The value of trade per capita in Andorra was greater than in the USA ($1 275.1), in Japan ($811.1), in Germany ($775.5), in France ($762.4), and in the USSR ($247.1). The growth of trade in Andorra was greater than in Germany (3.0%); but less than in Japan (8.2%), in the USSR (5.2%), in France (3.9%), and in the USA (3.9%).

The 1980s

The value of trade in Andorra was $206.6 million per year in the 1980s, ranked 125th in the world, and was on a par with Brunei ($204.2 million). The share in the world was 0.0098%, and 0.029% in Europe.

The share of trade in the economy of Andorra was 40.5% in the 1980s, ranked 2nd in the world.

The trade per capita in Andorra was $4 708.4 in the 1980s, ranked 4th in the world. The value of trade per capita in Andorra was greater than trade per capita in the world ($437.7) in 10.8 times, and was greater than trade per capita in Europe ($921.4) in 5.1 times.

The growth of trade in Andorra was 2.8% in the 1980s, ranked 96th in the world, and was on a par with Australia (2.7%), the Caribbean (2.8%), Zimbabwe (2.8%). The growth of trade in Andorra (2.8%) was less than growth of trade in the world (3.3%), was greater than growth of trade in Europe (1.9%).

Comparison with neighbors. The Andorra's trade was less than in France ($88.3 billion) and in Spain ($42.9 billion). The trade per capita in Andorra was greater than in France ($1 563.0) and in Spain ($1 111.7). The growth of trade in Andorra was greater than in France (2.6%) and in Spain (1.9%).

Comparison with leaders. The Andorran trade was less than in the USA ($653.3 billion), in Japan ($277.3 billion), in Germany ($116.7 billion), in the USSR ($112.3 billion), and in Italy ($95.7 billion). The trade per capita in Andorra was greater than in the USA ($2.7 thousand), in Japan ($2.3 thousand), in Italy ($1 684.2), in Germany ($1 496.0), and in the USSR ($408.1). The growth of trade in

Andorra was greater than in Italy (2.3%), in Germany (1.8%), and in the USSR (-0.62%); but less than in Japan (4.9%) and in the USA (4.4%).

The 1990s

The sector of trade in Andorra was $485.6 million per year in the 1990s, ranked 128th in the world. The share in the world was 0.012%, and 0.037% in Europe.

The share of trade in the economy of Andorra was 40.2% in the 1990s, ranked 2nd in the world, and was on a par with Monaco (39.9%).

The Andorran trade per capita was $7 899.2 in the 1990s, ranked 3rd in the world. The value of trade per capita in Andorra was greater than trade per capita in the world ($721.8) in 10.9 times, and was greater than trade per capita in Europe ($1 798.1) in 4.4 times.

The growth of trade in Andorra was 2.5% in the 1990s, ranked 120th in the world. The growth of trade in Andorra (2.5%) was less than growth of trade in the world (3.5%), was greater than growth of trade in Europe (2.0%).

Comparison with neighbors. The trade of Andorra was less than in France ($177.0 billion) and in Spain ($103.9 billion). The Andorran trade per capita was greater than in France ($3.0 thousand) and in Spain ($2.6 thousand). The growth of trade in Andorra was greater than in France (2.4%) and in Spain (1.9%).

Comparison with leaders. The value added of trade in Andorra was less than in the United States ($1.2 trillion), in Japan ($713.2 billion), in Germany ($243.7 billion), in Italy ($185.6 billion), and in France ($177.0 billion). The Andorra's trade per capita was greater than in Japan ($5.7 thousand), in the USA ($4.4 thousand), in Italy ($3.3 thousand), in Germany ($3.0 thousand), and in France ($3.0 thousand). The growth of trade in Andorra was greater than in France (2.4%) and in Italy (1.9%); but less than in the USA (4.3%), in Japan (3.8%), and in Germany (2.5%).

The 2000s

The sector of trade in Andorra was $698.9 million per year in the 2000s, ranked 138th in the world, and was on a par with New Caledonia ($705.6 million). The share in the world was 0.011%, and 0.035% in Europe.

The share of trade in the economy of Andorra was 27.2% in the 2000s, ranked 10th in the world.

The sector of trade per capita in Andorra was $9 159.0 in the 2000s, ranked 6th in the world. The value of trade per capita in Andorra was greater than trade per capita in the world ($990.3) in 9.2 times, and was greater than trade per capita in Europe ($2 771.1) in 3.3 times.

The growth of trade in Andorra was 0% in the 2000s, ranked 193rd in the world. The growth of trade in Andorra (0.018%) was less than growth of trade in the world (2.7%), was less than growth of trade in Europe (2.2%).

Comparison with neighbors. The Andorran trade was less than in France ($256.9 billion) and in Spain ($179.9 billion). The Andorra's trade per capita was greater than in Spain ($4.1 thousand) and in France ($4.1 thousand). The growth of trade in Andorra was less than in Spain (2.0%) and in France (1.2%).

Comparison with leaders. The trade of Andorra was less than in the USA ($1.9 trillion), in Japan ($771.8 billion), in Germany ($296.0 billion), in the UK ($293.5 billion), and in China ($262.0 billion). The Andorra's trade per capita was greater than in the USA ($6.4 thousand), in Japan ($6.0 thousand), in the UK ($4.9 thousand), in Germany ($3.6 thousand), and in China ($197.5). The growth of trade in Andorra was greater than in Japan (-0.77%); but less than in China (11.9%), in Germany (1.7%), in the United Kingdom (1.3%), and in the United States (1.1%).

The 2010s

The value of trade in Andorra was $712.5 million per year in the 2010s, ranked 160th in the world, and was on a par with French Polynesia ($713.0 million), South Sudan ($699.2 million). The share in the world was 0.0068%, and 0.026% in Europe.

The share of trade in the economy of Andorra was 25.1% in the 2010s, ranked 15th in the world.

The value of trade per capita in Andorra was $8 938.8 in the 2010s, ranked 9th in the world, and was on a par with the Cayman Islands ($8.7 thousand). The value of trade per capita in Andorra was greater than trade per capita in the world ($1 436.8) in 6.2 times, and was greater than trade per capita in Europe ($3 620.4) in 2.5 times.

The growth of trade in Andorra was -0.6% in the 2010s, ranked 193rd in the world. The growth of trade in Andorra (-0.60%) was less than growth of trade in the world (3.3%), was less than growth of trade in Europe (2.0%).

Comparison with neighbors. The Andorran trade was 442.7 times lower than in France ($315.4 billion) and 322.0 times lower than in Spain ($229.4 billion). The value added of trade per capita in Andorra was 82.4% higher than in Spain ($4.9 thousand) and 88.0% higher than in France ($4.8 thousand). The growth of trade in Andorra was less than in France (1.9%) and in Spain (1.6%).

Comparison with leaders. The value of trade in Andorra was 3 670.9 times lower than in the USA ($2.6 trillion), 1 676.4 times lower than in China ($1.2 trillion), 1 220.4 times lower than in Japan ($869.5 billion), 523.0 times lower than in Germany ($372.6 billion), and 463.1 times lower than in the United Kingdom ($330.0 billion). The Andorran trade per capita was 9.2% higher than in the USA ($8.2 thousand), 31.5% higher than in Japan ($6.8 thousand), 77.7% higher than in the United Kingdom ($5.0 thousand), 96.4% higher than in Germany ($4.6 thousand), and 10.5 times higher than in China ($851.7). The growth of trade in Andorra was less than in China (8.9%), in the United Kingdom (2.8%), in the USA (2.3%), in Germany (2.0%), and in Japan (0.77%).

Chapter IX. Services

(ISIC J-P)

The value of services in Andorra grew from $79.5 million per year in the 1970s to $1.6 billion per year in the 2010s, that is by $1.5 billion or 20.1 times. The change occurred at $1.3 billion due to a 4.8-fold increase in prices, as also at $119.5 million due to a 1.6-fold increase in productivity, as well as at $133.0 million due to the growing in population. The average annual growth in services is 3.5%. The minimum value of services was in 1970 at $30.7 million. The maximum value of services was in 2008 at $1.9 billion.

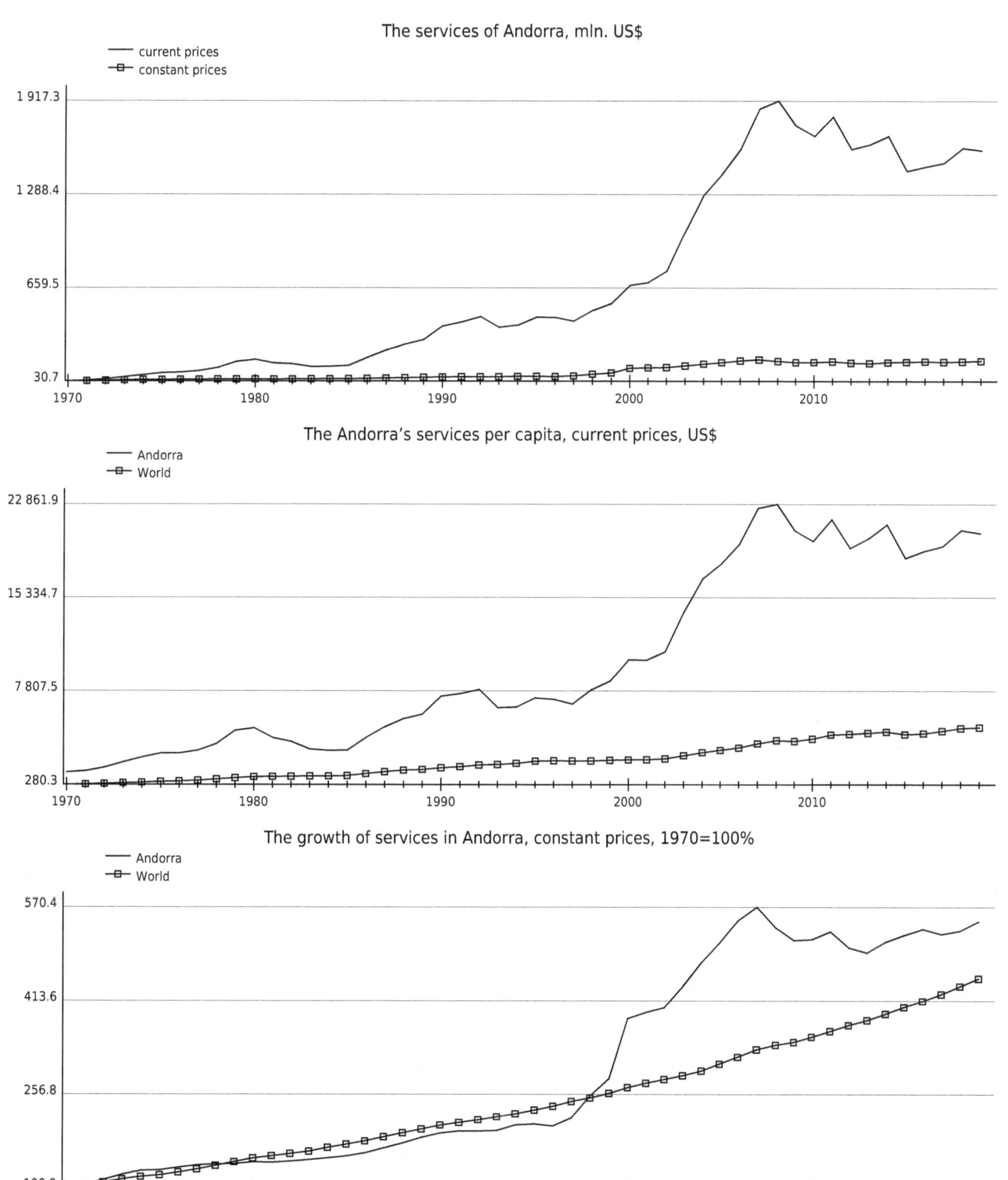

The services of Andorra, mln. US$

The Andorra's services per capita, current prices, US$

The growth of services in Andorra, constant prices, 1970=100%

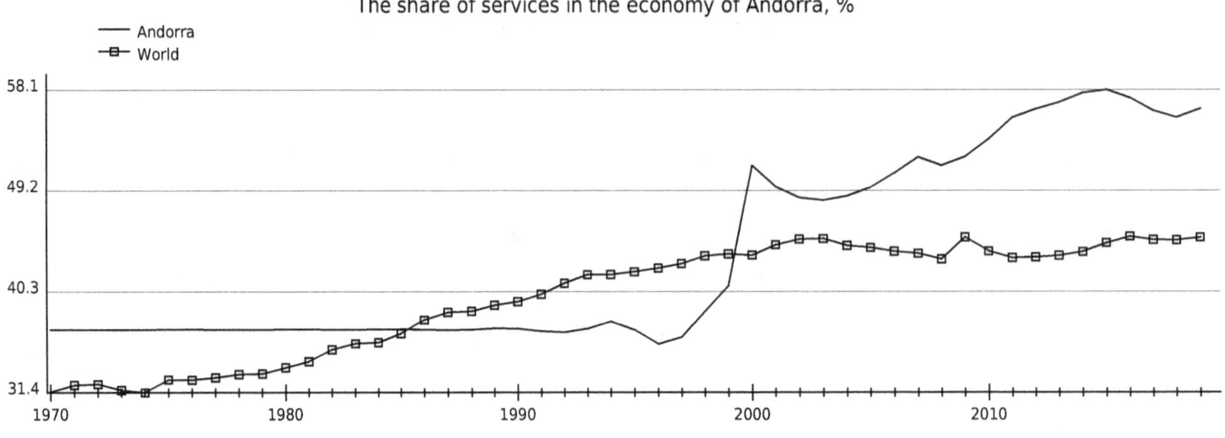

The 1970s

The value of services in Andorra was $79.5 million per year in the 1970s, ranked 144th in the world, and was on a par with Mali ($81.2 million). The share in the world was 0.0039%, and 0.0097% in Europe.

The share of services in the economy of Andorra was 36.9% in the 1970s, ranked 36th in the world, and was on a par with Barbados (36.9%), Canada (36.8%), Northern Europe (37.2%).

The Andorra's services per capita were $2 666.1 in the 1970s, ranked 11th in the world, and were on a par with the United Arab Emirates ($2.7 thousand), the Netherlands ($2.7 thousand), Qatar ($2.6 thousand). The value added of services per capita in Andorra was greater than services per capita in the world ($506.9) in 5.3 times, and was greater than services per capita in Europe ($1 130.2) in 2.4 times.

The growth of services in Andorra was 3.8% in the 1970s, ranked 126th in the world, and was on a par with Southern Africa (3.8%), Rwanda (3.8%), Norway (3.8%). The growth of services in Andorra (3.8%) was less than growth of services in the world (4.1%), was greater than growth of services in Europe (3.7%).

Comparison with neighbors. The Andorran services were less than in France ($121.8 billion) and in Spain ($27.2 billion). The sector of services per capita in Andorra was greater than in France ($2.3 thousand) and in Spain ($761.7). The growth of services in Andorra was less than in Spain (4.6%) and in France (3.9%).

Comparison with leaders. The services of Andorra were less than in the United States ($674.4 billion), in the USSR ($168.3 billion), in Japan ($153.8 billion), in Germany ($150.2 billion), and in France ($121.8 billion). The Andorra's services per capita were greater than in France ($2.3 thousand), in Germany ($1 907.6), in Japan ($1 381.3), and in the USSR ($667.3); but less than in the USA ($3.1 thousand). The growth of services in Andorra was greater than in the USA (3.3%) and in the USSR (0.90%); but less than in Japan (5.9%), in Germany (4.8%), and in France (3.9%).

The 1980s

The sector of services in Andorra was $188.2 million per year in the 1980s, ranked 146th in the world, and was on a par with Chad ($188.6 million), Sierra Leone ($190.1 million). The share in the world was 0.0035%, and 0.010% in Europe.

The share of services in the economy of Andorra was 36.9% in the 1980s, ranked 50th in the world, and was on a par with Vanuatu (36.9%), Palau (37.0%), Europe (36.8%).

The services per capita in Andorra were $4 289.9 in the 1980s, ranked 28th in the world, and were on a par with Finland ($4.4 thousand). The services per capita in Andorra were greater than services per capita in the world ($1 115.5) in 3.8 times, and were greater than services per capita in Europe ($2 449.2) by 75.2%.

The growth of services in Andorra was 2.8% in the 1980s, ranked 118th in the world, and was on a par with Canada (2.8%), North Korea (2.8%), Northern America (2.8%). The growth of services in Andorra (2.8%) was less than growth of services in the world (3.3%), was less than growth of services in Europe (3.0%).

Comparison with neighbors. The services of Andorra were less than in France ($294.5 billion) and in Spain ($76.2 billion). The value of services per capita in Andorra was greater than in Spain ($1 976.9); but less than in France ($5.2 thousand). The growth of services in

Andorra was greater than in France (2.3%); but less than in Spain (4.0%).

Comparison with leaders. The services of Andorra were less than in the United States ($1.9 trillion), in Japan ($619.9 billion), in Germany ($362.2 billion), in France ($294.5 billion), and in the UK ($265.4 billion). The Andorra's services per capita were less than in the USA ($7.8 thousand), in France ($5.2 thousand), in Japan ($5.1 thousand), in the UK ($4.7 thousand), and in Germany ($4.6 thousand). The growth of services in Andorra was greater than in France (2.3%); but less than in Japan (4.8%), in the UK (3.3%), in Germany (3.1%), and in the USA (2.8%).

The 1990s

The sector of services in Andorra was $451.5 million per year in the 1990s, ranked 152nd in the world, and was on a par with Cambodia ($446.9 million). The share in the world was 0.0039%, and 0.012% in Europe.

The share of services in the economy of Andorra was 37.4% in the 1990s, ranked 70th in the world, and was on a par with Guatemala (37.4%), the Maldives (37.3%), Japan (37.5%).

The value added of services per capita in Andorra was $7 344.9 in the 1990s, ranked 33rd in the world, and was on a par with Singapore ($7.3 thousand). The Andorra's services per capita were greater than services per capita in the world ($2 014.6) in 3.6 times, and were greater than services per capita in Europe ($5 286.9) by 38.9%.

The growth of services in Andorra was 4.4% in the 1990s, ranked 58th in the world, and was on a par with Saint Kitts and Nevis (4.4%), Oman (4.4%). The growth of services in Andorra (4.4%) was greater than growth of services in the world (2.7%), was greater than growth of services in Europe (2.1%).

Comparison with neighbors. The services of Andorra were less than in France ($628.2 billion) and in Spain ($197.5 billion). The value of services per capita in Andorra was greater than in Spain ($5.0 thousand); but less than in France ($10.6 thousand). The growth of services in Andorra was greater than in Spain (2.5%) and in France (1.6%).

Comparison with leaders. The Andorran services were less than in the United States ($3.8 trillion), in Japan ($1.6 trillion), in Germany ($908.0 billion), in France ($628.2 billion), and in the United Kingdom ($592.3 billion). The sector of services per capita in Andorra was less than in the USA ($14.4 thousand), in Japan ($12.8 thousand), in Germany ($11.3 thousand), in France ($10.6 thousand), and in the United Kingdom ($10.2 thousand). The growth of services in Andorra was greater than in Germany (3.2%), in the UK (3.0%), in the United States (2.3%), in Japan (1.7%), and in France (1.6%).

The 2000s

The services of Andorra were $1.3 billion per year in the 2000s, ranked 141st in the world, and were on a par with Kosovo ($1.3 billion). The share in the world was 0.0066%, and 0.020% in Europe.

The share of services in the economy of Andorra was 50.5% in the 2000s, ranked 17th in the world, and was on a par with the Americas (50.5%), Israel (50.6%), the Marshall Islands (50.3%).

The sector of services per capita in Andorra was $17 039.6 in the 2000s, ranked 16th in the world, and was on a par with Sweden ($16.9 thousand), Northern Europe ($16.8 thousand), Ireland ($17.5 thousand). The value of services per capita in Andorra was greater than services per capita in the world ($3 011.2) in 5.7 times, and was greater than services per capita in Europe ($8 787.5) by 93.9%.

The growth of services in Andorra was 6.2% in the 2000s, ranked 40th in the world, and was on a par with Kosovo (6.1%), Belize (6.1%), Pakistan (6.2%). The growth of services in Andorra (6.2%) was greater than growth of services in the world (2.9%), was greater than growth of services in Europe (2.0%).

Comparison with neighbors. The value of services in Andorra was less than in France ($997.0 billion) and in Spain ($404.5 billion). The value of services per capita in Andorra was greater than in France ($15.9 thousand) and in Spain ($9.3 thousand). The growth of services in Andorra was greater than in Spain (4.4%) and in France (1.5%).

Comparison with leaders. The value added of services in Andorra was less than in the USA ($6.7 trillion), in Japan ($2.0 trillion), in Germany ($1.2 trillion), in the UK ($1.1 trillion), and in France ($997.0 billion). The sector of services per capita in Andorra was greater than in France ($15.9 thousand), in Japan ($15.3 thousand), and in Germany ($15.0 thousand); but less than in the USA ($22.9 thousand) and in the United Kingdom ($18.0 thousand). The growth of services in Andorra was greater than in the UK (2.7%), in the United States (2.0%), in France (1.5%), in Japan (1.2%), and in Germany (0.57%).

The 2010s

The sector of services in Andorra was $1.6 billion per year in the 2010s, ranked 157th in the world, and was on a par with Mauritania ($1.6 billion). The share in the world was 0.0049%, and 0.018% in Europe.

The share of services in the economy of Andorra was 56.4% in the 2010s, ranked 9th in the world, and was on a par with Hong Kong (56.9%).

The sector of services per capita in Andorra was $20 057.6 in the 2010s, ranked 24th in the world, and was on a par with France ($20.2 thousand), Oceania ($20.2 thousand), Finland ($19.8 thousand). The Andorra's services per capita were greater than services per capita in the world ($4 467.8) in 4.5 times, and were greater than services per capita in Europe ($12 213.1) by 64.2%.

The growth of services in Andorra was 0.6% in the 2010s, ranked 186th in the world, and was on a par with North Korea (0.58%). The growth of services in Andorra (0.58%) was less than growth of services in the world (2.7%), was less than growth of services in Europe (1.3%).

Comparison with neighbors. The value of services in Andorra was 838.9 times lower than in France ($1.3 trillion) and 364.5 times lower than in Spain ($582.7 billion). The sector of services per capita in Andorra was 61.2% higher than in Spain ($12.4 thousand); but 0.81% lower than in France ($20.2 thousand). The growth of services in Andorra was less than in France (1.4%) and in Spain (1.2%).

Comparison with leaders. The value added of services in Andorra was 6 226.8 times lower than in the USA ($10.0 trillion), 2 218.6 times lower than in China ($3.5 trillion), 1 422.0 times lower than in Japan ($2.3 trillion), 1 005.5 times lower than in Germany ($1.6 trillion), and 847.9 times lower than in the UK ($1.4 trillion). The value added of services per capita in Andorra was 2.1% higher than in Germany ($19.6 thousand), 12.9% higher than in Japan ($17.8 thousand), and 7.9 times higher than in China ($2.5 thousand); but 35.6% lower than in the United States ($31.2 thousand) and 2.9% lower than in the UK ($20.7 thousand). The growth of services in Andorra was less than in China (8.4%), in the United States (1.8%), in the UK (1.7%), in Germany (1.2%), and in Japan (0.99%).

Part III. External relations

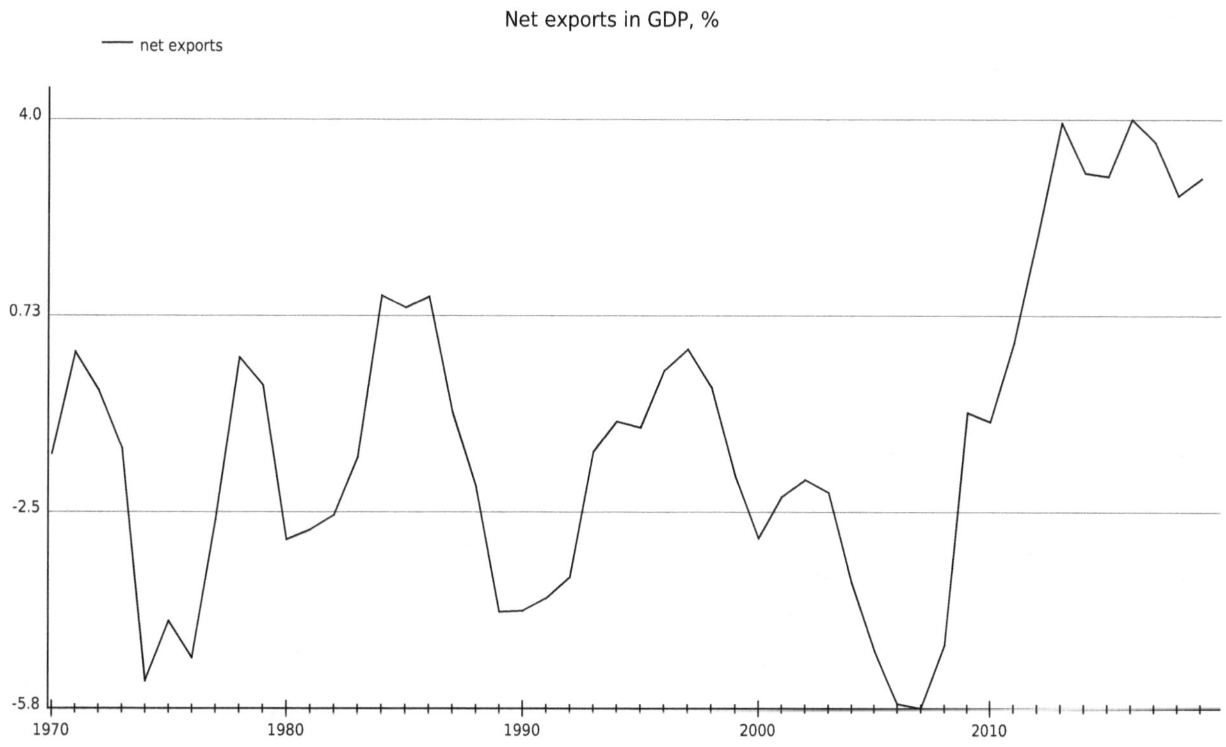

Chapter X. Exports

Exports of goods and services

The value of exports from Andorra rose from $34.1 million per year in the 1970s to $1.0 billion per year in the 2010s, that is by $997.8 million or 30.2 times. The change occurred at $815.0 million due to a 4.8-fold increase in prices, as also at $125.8 million due to a 2.4-fold increase in per capita rate, as well as at $57.0 million due to the rise in population. The average annual growth in exports is 4.7%. The minimum value of exports was in 1970 at $12.1 million. The maximum value of exports was in 2018 at $1.1 billion.

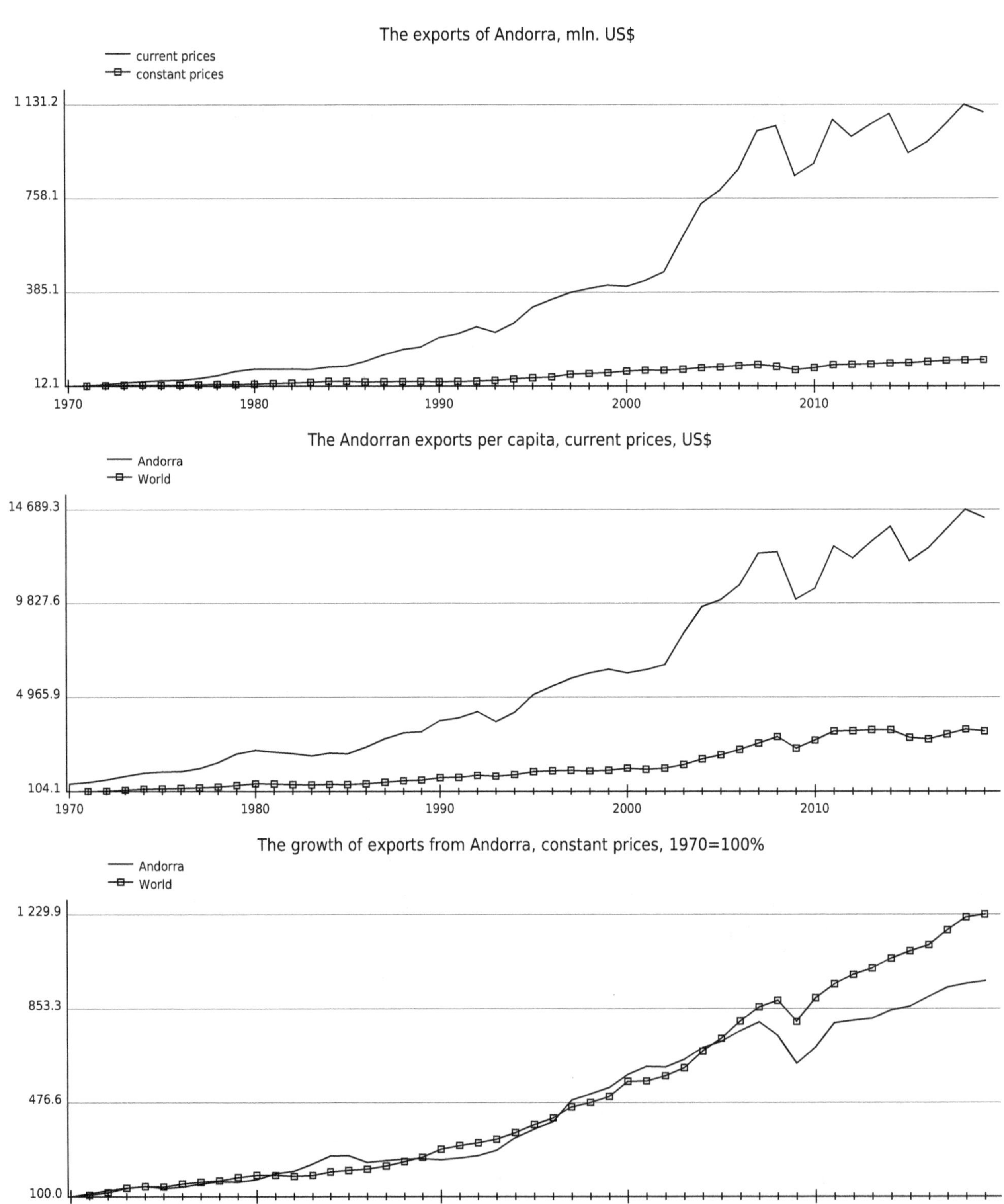

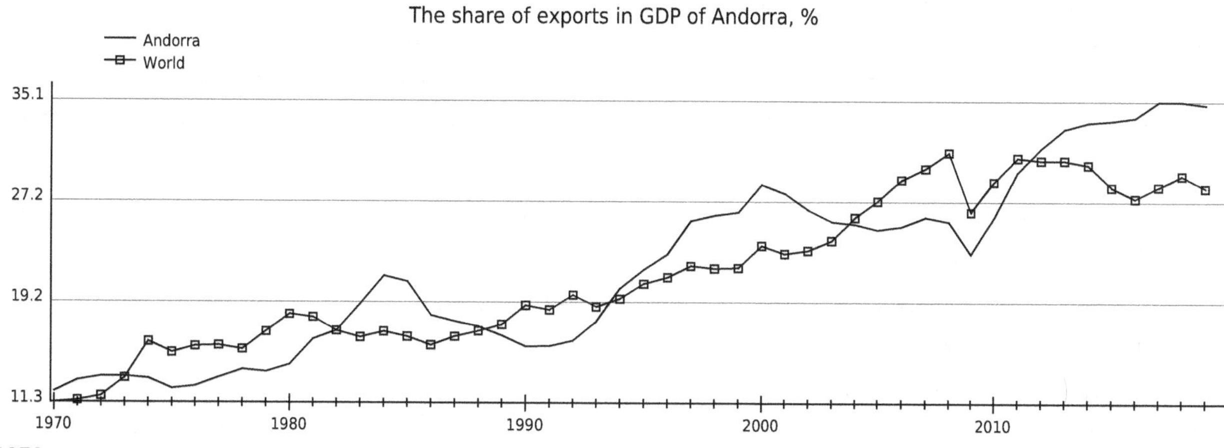

The 1970s

The Andorra's exports were $34.1 million per year in the 1970s, ranked 157th in the world, and were on a par with Belize ($34.9 million). The share in the world was 0.0035%, and 0.0073% from Europe.

The share of exports in GDP of Andorra was 13.2% in the 1970s, ranked 149th in the world, and was on a par with Spain (13.2%), Southern Asia (13.2%), Greece (13.2%).

The exports per capita from Andorra were $1 143.6 in the 1970s, ranked 41st in the world, and were on a par with Cyprus ($1 150.3), Israel ($1 166.0), Trinidad and Tobago ($1 166.3). The exports per capita from Andorra were greater than exports per capita in the world ($242.1) in 4.7 times, and were greater than exports per capita from Europe ($646.7) by 76.8%.

The growth of exports from Andorra was 5.2% in the 1970s, ranked 98th in the world. The growth of exports from Andorra (5.2%) was less than growth of exports in the world (6.5%), was less than growth of exports from Europe (6.1%).

Comparison with neighbors. The Andorra's exports were less than from France ($64.3 billion) and from Spain ($14.1 billion). The Andorra's exports per capita were greater than from Spain ($394.2); but less than from France ($1 199.1). The growth of exports from Andorra was less than from France (7.8%) and from Spain (7.6%).

Comparison with leaders. The exports of Andorra were less than from the United States ($128.0 billion), from Germany ($82.9 billion), from France ($64.3 billion), from Japan ($64.1 billion), and from the United Kingdom ($61.3 billion). The exports per capita from Andorra were greater than from the UK ($1 094.1), from Germany ($1 052.2), from the United States ($586.5), and from Japan ($575.8); but less than from France ($1 199.1). The growth of exports from Andorra was greater than from Germany (5.1%) and from the UK (5.0%); but less than from Japan (8.6%), from France (7.8%), and from the United States (6.8%).

The 1980s

The value of exports from Andorra was $107.4 million per year in the 1980s, ranked 154th in the world. The share in the world was 0.0042%, and 0.0092% from Europe.

The share of exports in GDP of Andorra was 17.6% in the 1980s, ranked 132nd in the world, and was on a par with Spain (17.6%), Greece (17.5%).

The exports per capita from Andorra were $2 449.0 in the 1980s, ranked 44th in the world, and were on a par with Gabon ($2.5 thousand). The exports per capita from Andorra were greater than exports per capita in the world ($529.9) in 4.6 times, and were greater than exports per capita from Europe ($1 521.7) by 60.9%.

The growth of exports from Andorra was 4.8% in the 1980s, ranked 74th in the world, and was on a par with Australia (4.8%). The growth of exports from Andorra (4.8%) was greater than growth of exports in the world (3.8%), was greater than growth of exports from Europe (4.0%).

Comparison with neighbors. The exports of Andorra were less than from France ($155.9 billion) and from Spain ($44.3 billion). The value of exports per capita from Andorra was greater than from Spain ($1 148.2); but less than from France ($2.8 thousand). The growth of exports from Andorra was greater than from France (4.0%); but less than from Spain (5.1%).

Comparison with leaders. The exports of Andorra were less than from the United States ($338.6 billion), from Japan ($210.6 billion), from Germany ($208.1 billion), from France ($155.9 billion), and from the United Kingdom ($155.0 billion). The Andorran exports per capita were greater than from Japan ($1 736.5) and from the USA ($1 413.8); but less than from France ($2.8 thousand), from the United Kingdom ($2.7 thousand), and from Germany ($2.7 thousand). The growth of exports from Andorra was greater than from Germany (4.7%), from France (4.0%), and from the UK (3.0%); but less than from Japan (6.7%) and from the United States (5.7%).

The 1990s

The value of exports from Andorra was $304.0 million per year in the 1990s, ranked 171st in the world. The share in the world was 0.0052%, and 0.011% from Europe.

The share of exports in GDP of Andorra was 21.1% in the 1990s, ranked 147th in the world, and was on a par with Western Africa (21.1%), Spain (21.0%), Egypt (20.9%).

The Andorran exports per capita were $4 944.8 in the 1990s, ranked 40th in the world, and were on a par with the Seychelles ($4.9 thousand), Slovenia ($4.9 thousand), Israel ($5.0 thousand). The value of exports per capita from Andorra was greater than exports per capita in the world ($1 029.5) in 4.8 times, and was greater than exports per capita from Europe ($3 810.5) by 29.8%.

The growth of exports from Andorra was 7.9% in the 1990s, ranked 57th in the world, and was on a par with Hong Kong (7.8%), Australia (7.9%), the Cook Islands (7.9%). The growth of exports from Andorra (7.9%) was greater than growth of exports in the world (6.9%), was greater than growth of exports from Europe (6.5%).

Comparison with neighbors. The value of exports from Andorra was less than from France ($329.8 billion) and from Spain ($124.1 billion). The value of exports per capita from Andorra was greater than from Spain ($3.1 thousand); but less than from France ($5.6 thousand). The growth of exports from Andorra was greater than from France (6.5%); but less than from Spain (9.4%).

Comparison with leaders. The Andorra's exports were less than from the United States ($773.6 billion), from Germany ($509.0 billion), from Japan ($418.7 billion), from France ($329.8 billion), and from the United Kingdom ($324.3 billion). The value of exports per capita from Andorra was greater than from Japan ($3.3 thousand) and from the United States ($2.9 thousand); but less than from Germany ($6.3 thousand), from the UK ($5.6 thousand), and from France ($5.6 thousand). The growth of exports from Andorra was greater than from the United States (7.2%), from France (6.5%), from Germany (6.0%), from the UK (5.7%), and from Japan (4.2%).

The 2000s

The Andorra's exports were $722.9 million per year in the 2000s, ranked 166th in the world, and were on a par with Malawi ($721.9 million). The share in the world was 0.0057%, and 0.013% from Europe.

The structure of exports: primary products (1.3%), resource-based manufactures (18.7%), low technology manufactures (26.1%), medium technology manufactures (41.5%), and high technology manufactures (6.9%).

Andorra exported goods to Spain (62.0%), France (17.9%), Germany (8.5%), Portugal (1.5%), Norway (1.4%) and other countries (8.7%).

The share of exports in GDP of Andorra was 25.5% in the 2000s, ranked 153rd in the world, and was on a par with Spain (25.5%), Cameroon (25.6%), the UK (25.5%).

The value of exports per capita from Andorra was $9 474.0 in the 2000s, ranked 39th in the world, and was on a par with Equatorial Guinea ($9.3 thousand). The Andorra's exports per capita were greater than exports per capita in the world ($1 933.7) in 4.9 times, and were greater than exports per capita from Europe ($7 642.0) by 24.0%.

The growth of exports from Andorra was 1.7% in the 2000s, ranked 161st in the world, and was on a par with Guatemala (1.7%). The growth of exports from Andorra (1.7%) was less than growth of exports in the world (4.8%), was less than growth of exports from Europe (3.8%).

Comparison with neighbors. The exports of Andorra were less than from France ($570.1 billion) and from Spain ($278.3 billion). The exports per capita from Andorra were greater than from France ($9.1 thousand) and from Spain ($6.4 thousand). The growth of exports from Andorra was less than from Spain (2.5%) and from France (2.3%).

Comparison with leaders. The value of exports from Andorra was less than from the USA ($1.3 trillion), from Germany ($1.0 trillion), from China ($780.2 billion), from Japan ($626.3 billion), and from the United Kingdom ($591.1 billion). The value of exports per capita from Andorra was greater than from Japan ($4.9 thousand), from the USA ($4.5 thousand), and from China ($588.1); but less than from Germany ($12.8 thousand) and from the United Kingdom ($9.8 thousand). The growth of exports from Andorra was less than from China (12.7%), from Germany (5.0%), from Japan (3.5%), from the USA (3.3%), and from the UK (2.8%).

The 2010s

The value of exports from Andorra was $1.0 billion per year in the 2010s, ranked 176th in the world, and was on a par with Lesotho ($1.0 billion). The share in the world was 0.0045%, and 0.011% from Europe.

The structure of exports: resource-based manufactures (6.7%), low technology manufactures (34.9%), medium technology manufactures (30.7%), and high technology manufactures (20.6%).

Andorra exported goods to Spain (51.1%), France (15.5%), Norway (4.1%), Switzerland (3.9%), the United States (3.3%) and other countries (22.0%).

The share of exports in GDP of Andorra was 32.5% in the 2010s, ranked 119th in the world, and was on a par with Costa Rica (32.5%), Syria (32.4%), Spain (32.5%).

The exports per capita from Andorra were $12 946.2 in the 2010s, ranked 42nd in the world, and were on a par with Australia ($12.9 thousand), South Korea ($13.0 thousand), Australasia ($12.7 thousand). The Andorra's exports per capita were greater than exports per capita in the world ($3 098.9) in 4.2 times, and were greater than exports per capita from Europe ($12 067.8) by 7.3%.

The growth of exports from Andorra was 4.3% in the 2010s, ranked 98th in the world, and was on a par with Southern Asia (4.2%), Austria (4.3%). The growth of exports from Andorra (4.3%) was less than growth of exports in the world (4.4%), was less than growth of exports from Europe (4.4%).

Comparison with neighbors. The exports of Andorra were 777.2 times lower than from France ($802.0 billion) and 425.8 times lower than from Spain ($439.4 billion). The value of exports per capita from Andorra was 7.1% higher than from France ($12.1 thousand) and 37.9% higher than from Spain ($9.4 thousand). The growth of exports from Andorra was greater than from France (4.0%); but less than from Spain (4.7%).

Comparison with leaders. The Andorran exports were 2 222.4 times lower than from China ($2.3 trillion), 2 199.5 times lower than from the United States ($2.3 trillion), 1 631.2 times lower than from Germany ($1.7 trillion), 832.9 times lower than from Japan ($859.4 billion), and 789.9 times lower than from the United Kingdom ($815.1 billion). The exports per capita from Andorra were 4.2% higher than from the United Kingdom ($12.4 thousand), 82.2% higher than from the United States ($7.1 thousand), 92.7% higher than from Japan ($6.7 thousand), and 7.9 times higher than from China ($1 635.3); but 37.0% lower than from Germany ($20.6 thousand). The growth of exports from Andorra was greater than from the United States (3.7%) and from the United Kingdom (3.1%); but less than from China (6.8%), from Germany (4.7%), and from Japan (4.6%).

Chapter XI. Imports

Imports of goods and services

The imports of Andorra enlarged from $39.6 million per year in the 1970s to $956.1 million per year in the 2010s, that is by $916.5 million or 24.2 times. The change occurred at $756.5 million due to a 4.8-fold increase in prices, as also at $93.9 million due to a 1.9-fold increase in per capita rate, as well as at $66.1 million due to the increase in population. The average annual growth in imports is 4.3%. The minimum value of imports was in 1970 at $13.6 million. The maximum value of imports was in 2007 at $1.3 billion.

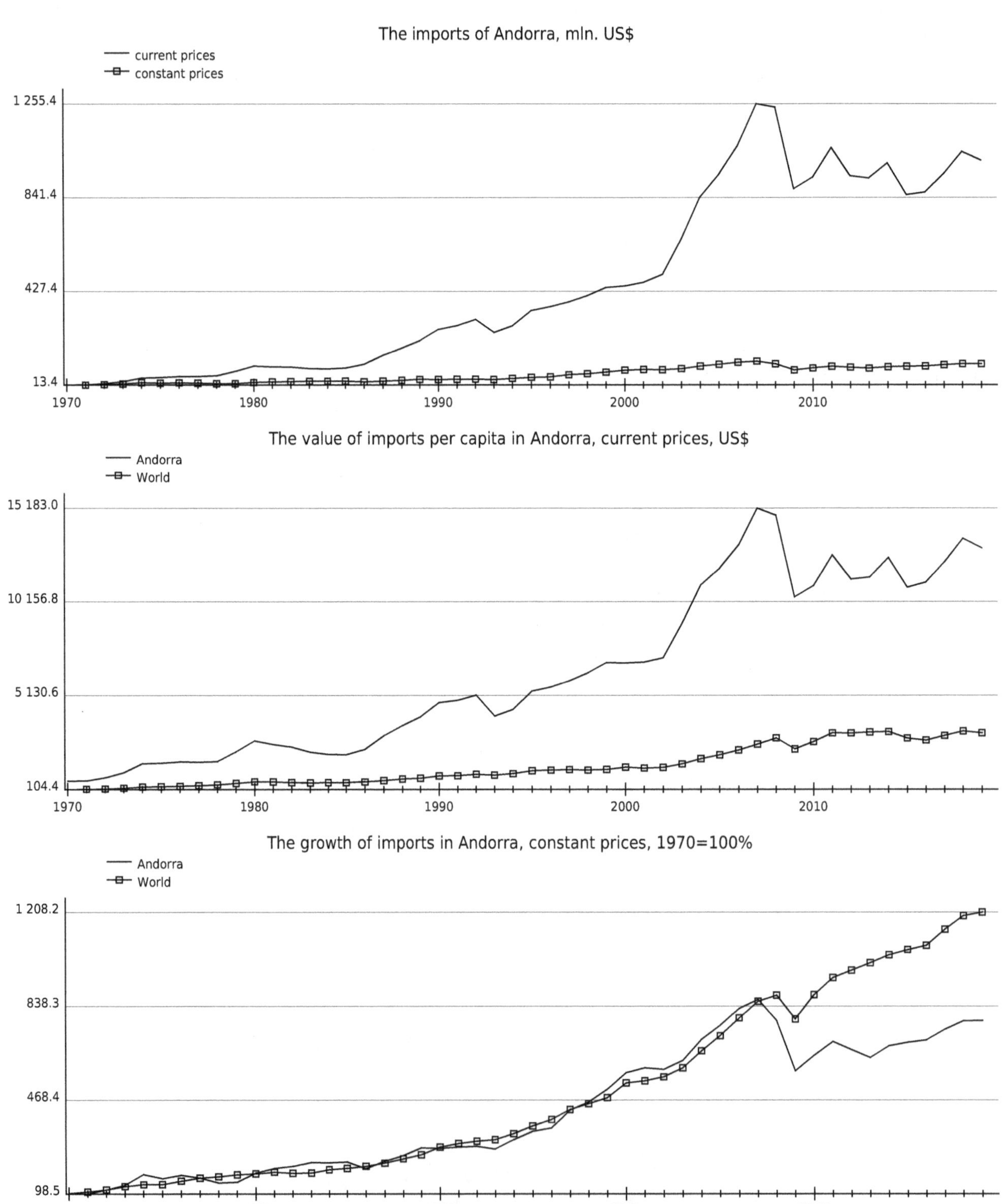

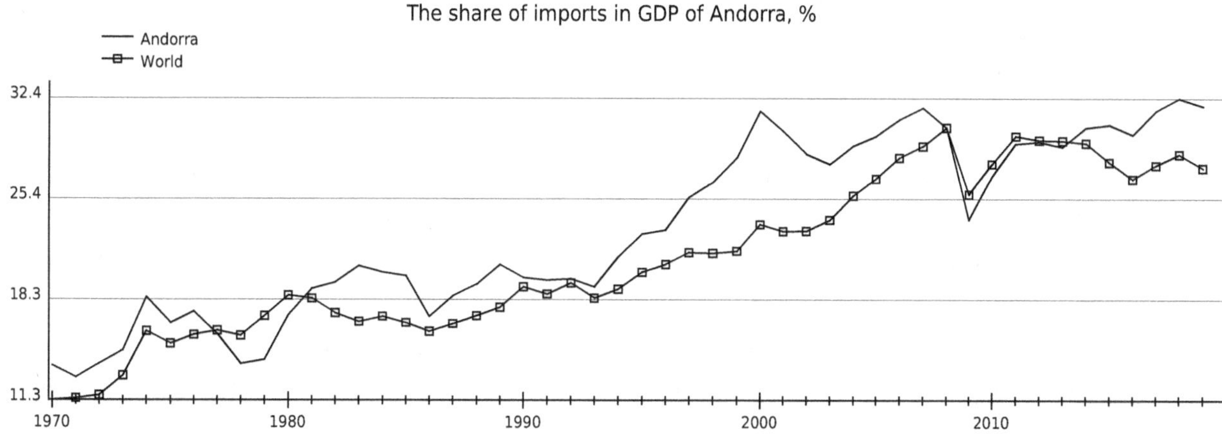

The 1970s

The imports of Andorra were $39.6 million per year in the 1970s, ranked 161st in the world. The share in the world was 0.0040%, and 0.0081% in Europe.

The share of imports in GDP of Andorra was 15.3% in the 1970s, ranked 158th in the world, and was on a par with Spain (15.3%).

The Andorra's imports per capita were $1 326.1 in the 1970s, ranked 39th in the world. The imports per capita in Andorra were greater than imports per capita in the world ($244.3) in 5.4 times, and were greater than imports per capita in Europe ($672.3) by 97.2%.

The growth of imports in Andorra was 4.2% in the 1970s, ranked 122nd in the world, and was on a par with Guyana (4.1%), Northern Europe (4.1%), Albania (4.2%). The growth of imports in Andorra (4.2%) was less than growth of imports in the world (6.3%), was less than growth of imports in Europe (5.4%).

Comparison with neighbors. The value of imports in Andorra was less than in France ($63.3 billion) and in Spain ($16.3 billion). The value of imports per capita in Andorra was greater than in France ($1 181.1) and in Spain ($457.1). The growth of imports in Andorra was less than in France (7.2%) and in Spain (6.7%).

Comparison with leaders. The value of imports in Andorra was less than in the United States ($133.2 billion), in Germany ($92.5 billion), in France ($63.3 billion), in the UK ($62.4 billion), and in Japan ($61.0 billion). The Andorran imports per capita were greater than in France ($1 181.1), in Germany ($1 175.1), in the UK ($1 113.2), in the United States ($610.4), and in Japan ($547.6). The growth of imports in Andorra was less than in France (7.2%), in Japan (7.0%), in Germany (5.6%), in the USA (5.1%), and in the United Kingdom (4.5%).

The 1980s

The imports of Andorra were $117.7 million per year in the 1980s, ranked 159th in the world. The share in the world was 0.0045%, and 0.0099% in Europe.

The share of imports in GDP of Andorra was 19.3% in the 1980s, ranked 149th in the world, and was on a par with Spain (19.3%), Mozambique (19.3%), Oceania (19.1%).

The value of imports per capita in Andorra was $2 683.9 in the 1980s, ranked 45th in the world. The value of imports per capita in Andorra was greater than imports per capita in the world ($539.1) in 5.0 times, and was greater than imports per capita in Europe ($1 550.8) by 73.1%.

The growth of imports in Andorra was 6.8% in the 1980s, ranked 31st in the world, and was on a par with Australia (6.8%). The growth of imports in Andorra (6.8%) was greater than growth of imports in the world (3.8%), was greater than growth of imports in Europe (4.1%).

Comparison with neighbors. The Andorran imports were less than in France ($162.0 billion) and in Spain ($48.5 billion). The value of imports per capita in Andorra was greater than in Spain ($1 258.3); but less than in France ($2.9 thousand). The growth of imports in Andorra was greater than in France (4.3%); but less than in Spain (8.1%).

Comparison with leaders. The imports of Andorra were less than in the USA ($417.2 billion), in Germany ($225.6 billion), in Japan ($175.9 billion), in France ($162.0 billion), and in the UK ($157.7 billion). The value of imports per capita in Andorra was greater than in the United States ($1 742.4) and in Japan ($1 450.4); but less than in Germany ($2.9 thousand), in France ($2.9 thousand), and in the United Kingdom ($2.8 thousand). The growth of imports in Andorra was greater than in the United States (5.8%), in the United Kingdom (5.1%), in Japan (4.6%), in France (4.3%), and in Germany (3.3%).

The 1990s

The value of imports in Andorra was $329.2 million per year in the 1990s, ranked 178th in the world, and was on a par with the Central African Republic ($324.4 million). The share in the world was 0.0057%, and 0.012% in Europe.

The share of imports in GDP of Andorra was 22.8% in the 1990s, ranked 172nd in the world, and was on a par with Kenya (22.8%), Spain (22.8%), Southern Africa (22.7%).

The value of imports per capita in Andorra was $5 354.3 in the 1990s, ranked 41st in the world. The Andorra's imports per capita were greater than imports per capita in the world ($1 015.5) in 5.3 times, and were greater than imports per capita in Europe ($3 655.2) by 46.5%.

The growth of imports in Andorra was 6.2% in the 1990s, ranked 75th in the world, and was on a par with Bolivia (6.2%). The growth of imports in Andorra (6.2%) was less than growth of imports in the world (6.6%), was greater than growth of imports in Europe (5.9%).

Comparison with neighbors. The imports of Andorra were less than in France ($308.5 billion) and in Spain ($134.4 billion). The value of imports per capita in Andorra was greater than in France ($5.2 thousand) and in Spain ($3.4 thousand). The growth of imports in Andorra was greater than in France (5.1%); but less than in Spain (9.1%).

Comparison with leaders. The imports of Andorra were less than in the USA ($874.1 billion), in Germany ($501.6 billion), in Japan ($355.9 billion), in the United Kingdom ($330.2 billion), and in France ($308.5 billion). The value of imports per capita in Andorra was greater than in France ($5.2 thousand), in the United States ($3.3 thousand), and in Japan ($2.8 thousand); but less than in Germany ($6.2 thousand) and in the UK ($5.7 thousand). The growth of imports in Andorra was greater than in France (5.1%), in the UK (5.1%), and in Japan (3.3%); but less than in the USA (8.3%) and in Germany (6.4%).

The 2000s

The imports of Andorra were $830.3 million per year in the 2000s, ranked 173rd in the world, and were on a par with the Seychelles ($844.4 million). The share in the world was 0.0067%, and 0.016% in Europe.

The structure of imports: primary products (5.4%), resource-based manufactures (20.8%), low technology manufactures (23.4%), medium technology manufactures (28.1%), and high technology manufactures (8.5%).

Andorra imported goods from Spain (65.4%), France (22.9%), Germany (2.6%), Italy (2.3%), the UK (1.4%) and other countries (5.3%).

The share of imports in GDP of Andorra was 29.3% in the 2000s, ranked 163rd in the world, and was on a par with Spain (29.3%).

The imports per capita in Andorra were $10 881.6 in the 2000s, ranked 36th in the world, and were on a par with New Caledonia ($11.0 thousand), Slovenia ($10.8 thousand), the UK ($10.6 thousand). The imports per capita in Andorra were greater than imports per capita in the world ($1 899.9) in 5.7 times, and were greater than imports per capita in Europe ($7 287.7) by 49.3%.

The growth of imports in Andorra was 1.3% in the 2000s, ranked 186th in the world, and was on a par with Palestine (1.3%), Somalia (1.3%). The growth of imports in Andorra (1.3%) was less than growth of imports in the world (5.1%), was less than growth of imports in Europe (4.0%).

Comparison with neighbors. The value of imports in Andorra was less than in France ($566.1 billion) and in Spain ($319.1 billion). The value of imports per capita in Andorra was greater than in France ($9.0 thousand) and in Spain ($7.3 thousand). The growth of imports in Andorra was less than in France (3.5%) and in Spain (2.8%).

Comparison with leaders. The Andorran imports were less than in the United States ($1.9 trillion), in Germany ($914.7 billion), in the UK ($641.8 billion), in China ($641.1 billion), and in Japan ($566.4 billion). The imports per capita in Andorra were greater than in the UK ($10.6 thousand), in the USA ($6.4 thousand), in Japan ($4.4 thousand), and in China ($483.3); but less than in Germany ($11.2 thousand). The growth of imports in Andorra was less than in China (15.1%), in Germany (3.7%), in the United Kingdom (3.1%), in the United States (2.8%), and in Japan (1.8%).

The 2010s

The value of imports in Andorra was $956.1 million per year in the 2010s, ranked 182nd in the world. The share in the world was

0.0043%, and 0.012% in Europe.

The structure of imports: primary products (7.6%), resource-based manufactures (28.2%), low technology manufactures (23.2%), medium technology manufactures (27.7%), and high technology manufactures (9.2%).

Andorra imported goods from Spain (68.4%), France (18.9%), Germany (3.1%), Italy (1.5%), the Netherlands (1.3%) and other countries (6.8%).

The share of imports in GDP of Andorra was 30.1% in the 2010s, ranked 169th in the world, and was on a par with Spain (30.1%), Africa (29.9%), Chad (29.9%).

The imports per capita in Andorra were $11 995.0 in the 2010s, ranked 47th in the world, and were on a par with Israel ($11.8 thousand), Republic of Korea ($11.8 thousand). The imports per capita in Andorra were greater than imports per capita in the world ($3 015.6) in 4.0 times, and were greater than imports per capita in Europe ($11 149.4) by 7.6%.

The growth of imports in Andorra was 3% in the 2010s, ranked 142nd in the world, and was on a par with the TCI (3.0%), Liechtenstein (3.0%). The growth of imports in Andorra (3.0%) was less than growth of imports in the world (4.4%), was less than growth of imports in Europe (4.3%).

Comparison with neighbors. The value of imports in Andorra was 870.1 times lower than in France ($831.9 billion) and 425.5 times lower than in Spain ($406.8 billion). The Andorra's imports per capita were 38.0% higher than in Spain ($8.7 thousand); but 4.4% lower than in France ($12.5 thousand). The growth of imports in Andorra was greater than in Spain (2.5%); but less than in France (4.1%).

Comparison with leaders. The imports of Andorra were 2 946.6 times lower than in the United States ($2.8 trillion), 2 164.1 times lower than in China ($2.1 trillion), 1 521.5 times lower than in Germany ($1.5 trillion), 918.2 times lower than in Japan ($877.9 billion), and 894.0 times lower than in the UK ($854.8 billion). The Andorra's imports per capita were 36.0% higher than in the United States ($8.8 thousand), 74.8% higher than in Japan ($6.9 thousand), and 8.1 times higher than in China ($1 475.4); but 32.5% lower than in Germany ($17.8 thousand) and 7.9% lower than in the United Kingdom ($13.0 thousand). The growth of imports in Andorra was less than in China (8.2%), in Germany (4.8%), in the United States (4.4%), in Japan (3.8%), and in the UK (3.6%).

Part IV. Consumption

Chapter XII. Government consumption expenditure

General government final consumption expenditure

The government expenditure of Andorra enlarged from $29.7 million per year in the 1970s to $622.3 million per year in the 2010s, that is by $592.6 million or 20.9 times. The change occurred at $488.7 million due to a 4.7-fold increase in prices, as also at $54.2 million due to a 1.7-fold increase in per capita rate, as well as at $49.7 million due to the expansion in population. The average annual growth in government expenditure is 3.9%. The minimum value of government consumption expenditure was in 1970 at $9.8 million. The maximum value of government consumption expenditure was in 2008 at $769.1 million.

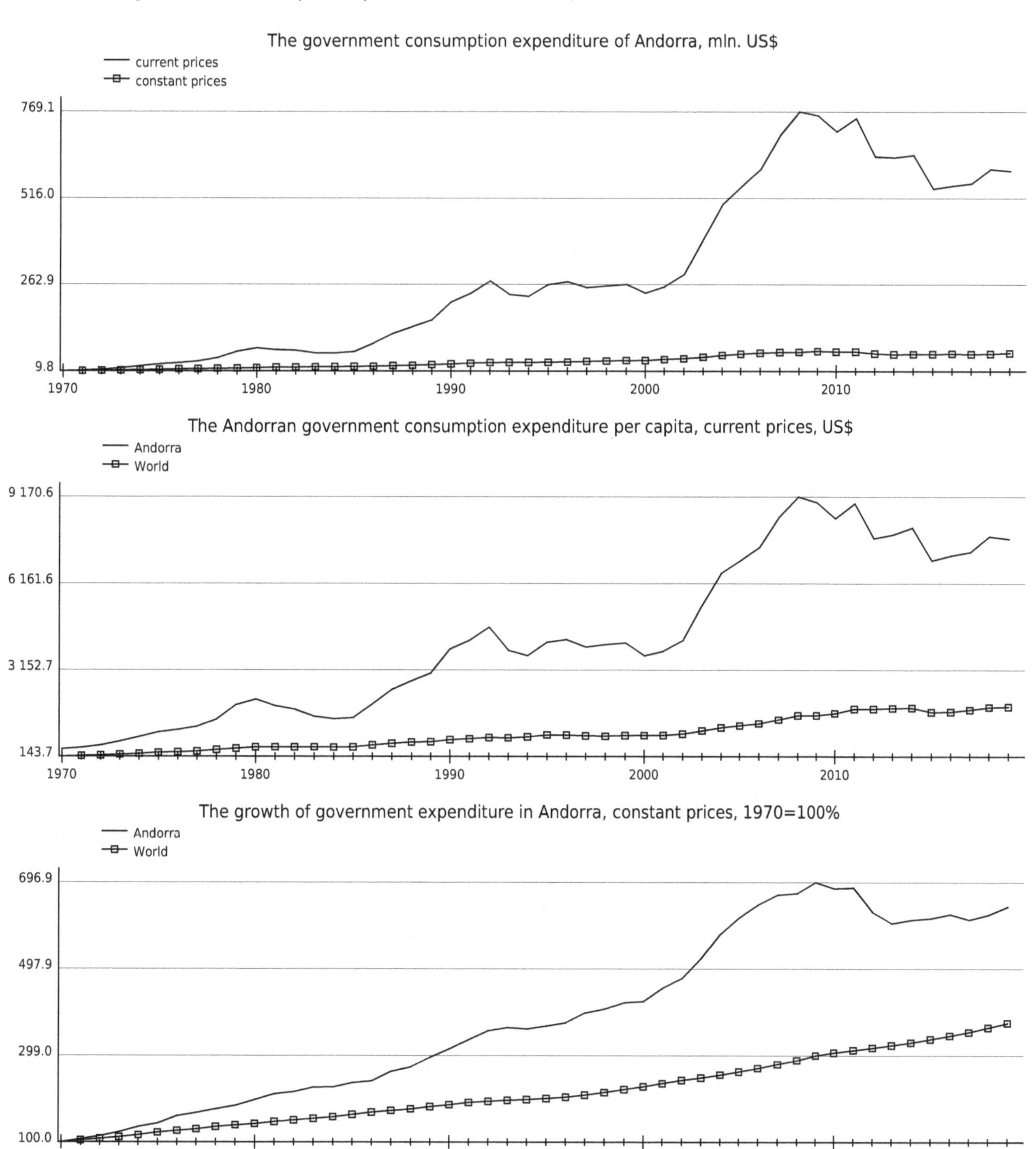

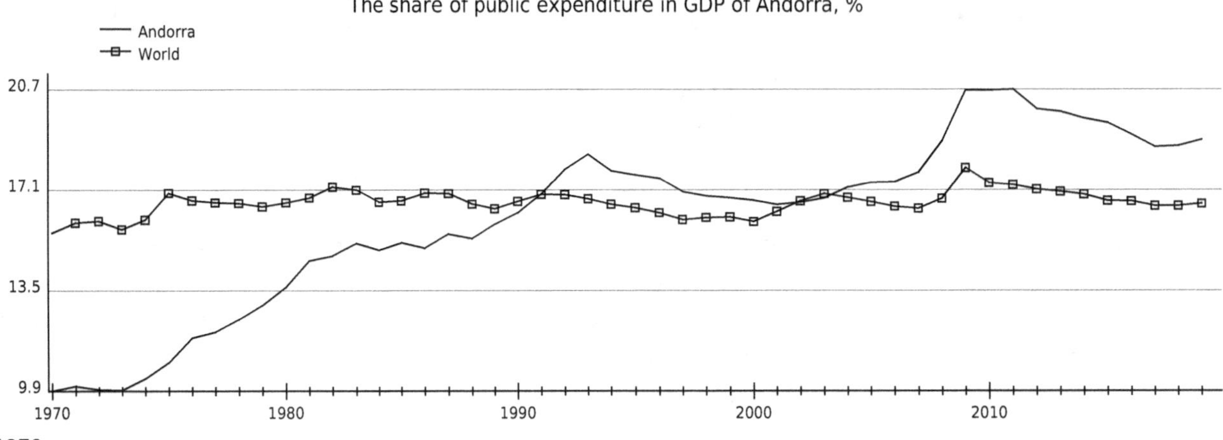

The 1970s

The public expenditure of Andorra was $29.7 million per year in the 1970s, ranked 150th in the world, and was on a par with Liechtenstein ($29.2 million), the Comoros ($30.4 million). The share in the world was 0.0028%, and 0.0060% in Europe.

The share of government expenditure in GDP of Andorra was 11.5% in the 1970s, ranked 138th in the world, and was on a par with Spain (11.5%), Thailand (11.5%).

The Andorra's public expenditure per capita was $996.8 in the 1970s, ranked 25th in the world. The government consumption expenditure per capita in Andorra was greater than public expenditure per capita in the world ($265.2) in 3.8 times, and was greater than government consumption expenditure per capita in Europe ($678.9) by 46.8%.

The growth of government consumption expenditure in Andorra was 7% in the 1970s, ranked 62nd in the world, and was on a par with Asia (6.9%), Greece (6.9%), Singapore (6.9%). The growth of government consumption expenditure in Andorra (7.0%) was greater than growth of government consumption expenditure in the world (3.7%), was greater than growth of government expenditure in Europe (4.5%).

Comparison with neighbors. The Andorra's public expenditure was less than in France ($64.5 billion) and in Spain ($12.3 billion). The government expenditure per capita in Andorra was greater than in Spain ($343.6); but less than in France ($1 202.3). The growth of government consumption expenditure in Andorra was greater than in Spain (5.6%) and in France (5.0%).

Comparison with leaders. The Andorra's public expenditure was less than in the USA ($285.9 billion), in the USSR ($117.3 billion), in Germany ($95.6 billion), in Japan ($78.0 billion), and in France ($64.5 billion). The Andorra's government expenditure per capita was greater than in Japan ($700.2) and in the USSR ($465.0); but less than in the USA ($1 310.2), in Germany ($1 213.7), and in France ($1 202.3). The growth of public expenditure in Andorra was greater than in Japan (5.3%), in France (5.0%), in Germany (4.4%), and in the USA (0.94%); but less than in the USSR (7.2%).

The 1980s

The Andorra's public expenditure was $92.1 million per year in the 1980s, ranked 149th in the world, and was on a par with Guinea-Bissau ($92.3 million). The share in the world was 0.0036%, and 0.0085% in Europe.

The share of government expenditure in GDP of Andorra was 15.1% in the 1980s, ranked 111th in the world, and was on a par with Spain (15.1%), Tonga (15.1%), Ethiopia (15.0%).

The government expenditure per capita in Andorra was $2 098.9 in the 1980s, ranked 33rd in the world, and was on a par with Japan ($2.1 thousand), Libya ($2.1 thousand). The public expenditure per capita in Andorra was greater than government consumption expenditure per capita in the world ($523.5) in 4.0 times, and was greater than government consumption expenditure per capita in Europe ($1 404.9) by 49.4%.

The growth of government consumption expenditure in Andorra was 4.9% in the 1980s, ranked 54th in the world, and was on a par with Iraq (4.8%), Iceland (4.9%), Malta (4.9%). The growth of public expenditure in Andorra (4.9%) was greater than growth of public expenditure in the world (2.7%), was greater than growth of government expenditure in Europe (2.3%).

Comparison with neighbors. The Andorran public expenditure was less than in France ($159.8 billion) and in Spain ($37.9 billion). The

Andorra's government consumption expenditure per capita was greater than in Spain ($984.1); but less than in France ($2.8 thousand). The growth of public expenditure in Andorra was greater than in Spain (4.7%) and in France (2.8%).

Comparison with leaders. The government consumption expenditure of Andorra was less than in the USA ($665.3 billion), in Japan ($257.4 billion), in Germany ($203.7 billion), in the USSR ($181.1 billion), and in France ($159.8 billion). The government consumption expenditure per capita in Andorra was greater than in the USSR ($658.0); but less than in France ($2.8 thousand), in the United States ($2.8 thousand), in Germany ($2.6 thousand), and in Japan ($2.1 thousand). The growth of public expenditure in Andorra was greater than in Japan (3.5%), in France (2.8%), in the United States (2.6%), and in Germany (0.98%); but less than in the USSR (5.4%).

The 1990s

The government consumption expenditure of Andorra was $249.3 million per year in the 1990s, ranked 157th in the world, and was on a par with Mongolia ($243.6 million). The share in the world was 0.0053%, and 0.013% in Europe.

The share of public expenditure in GDP of Andorra was 17.3% in the 1990s, ranked 95th in the world, and was on a par with Spain (17.3%), Saint Vincent and the Grenadines (17.3%), Portugal (17.3%).

The Andorran government consumption expenditure per capita was $4 055.5 in the 1990s, ranked 28th in the world, and was on a par with the United Kingdom ($4.1 thousand). The Andorran government expenditure per capita was greater than government expenditure per capita in the world ($824.8) in 4.9 times, and was greater than public expenditure per capita in Europe ($2 620.7) by 54.7%.

The growth of government expenditure in Andorra was 3.6% in the 1990s, ranked 63rd in the world, and was on a par with Guinea-Bissau (3.6%), Nepal (3.6%). The growth of government consumption expenditure in Andorra (3.6%) was greater than growth of government consumption expenditure in the world (2.0%), was greater than growth of government expenditure in Europe (1.3%).

Comparison with neighbors. The government consumption expenditure of Andorra was less than in France ($325.4 billion) and in Spain ($102.0 billion). The government expenditure per capita in Andorra was greater than in Spain ($2.6 thousand); but less than in France ($5.5 thousand). The growth of public expenditure in Andorra was greater than in Spain (3.2%) and in France (1.8%).

Comparison with leaders. The government consumption expenditure of Andorra was less than in the United States ($1.1 trillion), in Japan ($651.8 billion), in Germany ($419.6 billion), in France ($325.4 billion), and in the United Kingdom ($234.6 billion). The government consumption expenditure per capita in Andorra was greater than in the UK ($4.1 thousand); but less than in France ($5.5 thousand), in Germany ($5.2 thousand), in Japan ($5.2 thousand), and in the USA ($4.3 thousand). The growth of public expenditure in Andorra was greater than in Japan (3.0%), in Germany (2.4%), in the United Kingdom (2.1%), in France (1.8%), and in the USA (1.3%).

The 2000s

The Andorra's government consumption expenditure was $505.5 million per year in the 2000s, ranked 150th in the world, and was on a par with Montenegro ($496.0 million), Mauritania ($516.9 million). The share in the world was 0.0065%, and 0.017% in Europe.

The share of government consumption expenditure in GDP of Andorra was 17.8% in the 2000s, ranked 73rd in the world, and was on a par with Kyrgyzstan (17.9%), Spain (17.9%), Oceania (17.8%).

The government consumption expenditure per capita in Andorra was $6 624.0 in the 2000s, ranked 23rd in the world, and was on a par with French Polynesia ($6.6 thousand), Japan ($6.6 thousand), New Caledonia ($6.7 thousand). The government expenditure per capita in Andorra was greater than government consumption expenditure per capita in the world ($1 200.9) in 5.5 times, and was greater than government consumption expenditure per capita in Europe ($4 171.1) by 58.8%.

The growth of public expenditure in Andorra was 5.2% in the 2000s, ranked 66th in the world, and was on a par with Western Asia (5.1%), Eastern Asia (5.1%), Thailand (5.2%). The growth of government expenditure in Andorra (5.2%) was greater than growth of government consumption expenditure in the world (3.1%), was greater than growth of public expenditure in Europe (2.1%).

Comparison with neighbors. The government consumption expenditure of Andorra was less than in France ($479.9 billion) and in Spain ($194.8 billion). The government consumption expenditure per capita in Andorra was greater than in Spain ($4.5 thousand); but less than in France ($7.6 thousand). The growth of government consumption expenditure in Andorra was greater than in Spain (5.0%) and in France (1.7%).

Comparison with leaders. The government expenditure of Andorra was less than in the United States ($1.9 trillion), in Japan ($844.2 billion), in Germany ($520.1 billion), in France ($479.9 billion), and in the United Kingdom ($453.4 billion). The Andorra's government consumption expenditure per capita was greater than in Japan ($6.6 thousand), in the United States ($6.5 thousand), and in Germany ($6.4 thousand); but less than in France ($7.6 thousand) and in the United Kingdom ($7.5 thousand). The growth of public expenditure in Andorra was greater than in the UK (2.9%), in the United States (2.2%), in Japan (1.7%), in France (1.7%), and in Germany (1.4%).

The 2010s

The government consumption expenditure of Andorra was $622.3 million per year in the 2010s, ranked 167th in the world, and was on a par with Malawi ($622.4 million). The share in the world was 0.0048%, and 0.015% in Europe.

The share of government consumption expenditure in GDP of Andorra was 19.6% in the 2010s, ranked 58th in the world, and was on a par with Spain (19.6%), Montenegro (19.6%), Iraq (19.5%).

The public expenditure per capita in Andorra was $7 807.3 in the 2010s, ranked 28th in the world, and was on a par with Oceania ($7.9 thousand). The government consumption expenditure per capita in Andorra was greater than public expenditure per capita in the world ($1 785.1) in 4.4 times, and was greater than public expenditure per capita in Europe ($5 705.5) by 36.8%.

The growth of public expenditure in Andorra was -0.8% in the 2010s, ranked 197th in the world, and was on a par with Anguilla (-0.84%), Portugal (-0.83%). The growth of public expenditure in Andorra (-0.83%) was less than growth of government expenditure in the world (2.3%), was less than growth of government expenditure in Europe (0.99%).

Comparison with neighbors. The Andorran government expenditure was 1 025.0 times lower than in France ($637.9 billion) and 424.6 times lower than in Spain ($264.2 billion). The government expenditure per capita in Andorra was 38.3% higher than in Spain ($5.6 thousand); but 18.8% lower than in France ($9.6 thousand). The growth of government expenditure in Andorra was less than in France (1.3%) and in Spain (0.32%).

Comparison with leaders. The Andorran government consumption expenditure was 4 263.7 times lower than in the USA ($2.7 trillion), 2 698.2 times lower than in China ($1.7 trillion), 1 676.0 times lower than in Japan ($1.0 trillion), 1 159.5 times lower than in Germany ($721.6 billion), and 1 025.0 times lower than in France ($637.9 billion). The government expenditure per capita in Andorra was 6.5 times higher than in China ($1 197.3); but 18.8% lower than in France ($9.6 thousand), 11.4% lower than in Germany ($8.8 thousand), 6.0% lower than in the USA ($8.3 thousand), and 4.2% lower than in Japan ($8.2 thousand). The growth of government expenditure in Andorra was less than in China (8.3%), in Germany (1.9%), in Japan (1.3%), in France (1.3%), and in the United States (0.0052%).

Chapter XIII. Household consumption expenditure

(including Non-profit institutions serving households)

The household expenditure of Andorra enlarged from $165.6 million per year in the 1970s to $1.9 billion per year in the 2010s, that is by $1.7 billion or 11.2 times. The change occurred at $1.5 billion due to a 4.8-fold increase in prices, as also at -$56.4 million due to a 1.1-fold decrease in per capita rate, as well as at $276.9 million due to the increase in population. The average annual growth in household consumption expenditure is 2.3%. The minimum value of household consumption expenditure was in 1970 at $63.5 million. The maximum value of household consumption expenditure was in 2008 at $2.3 billion.

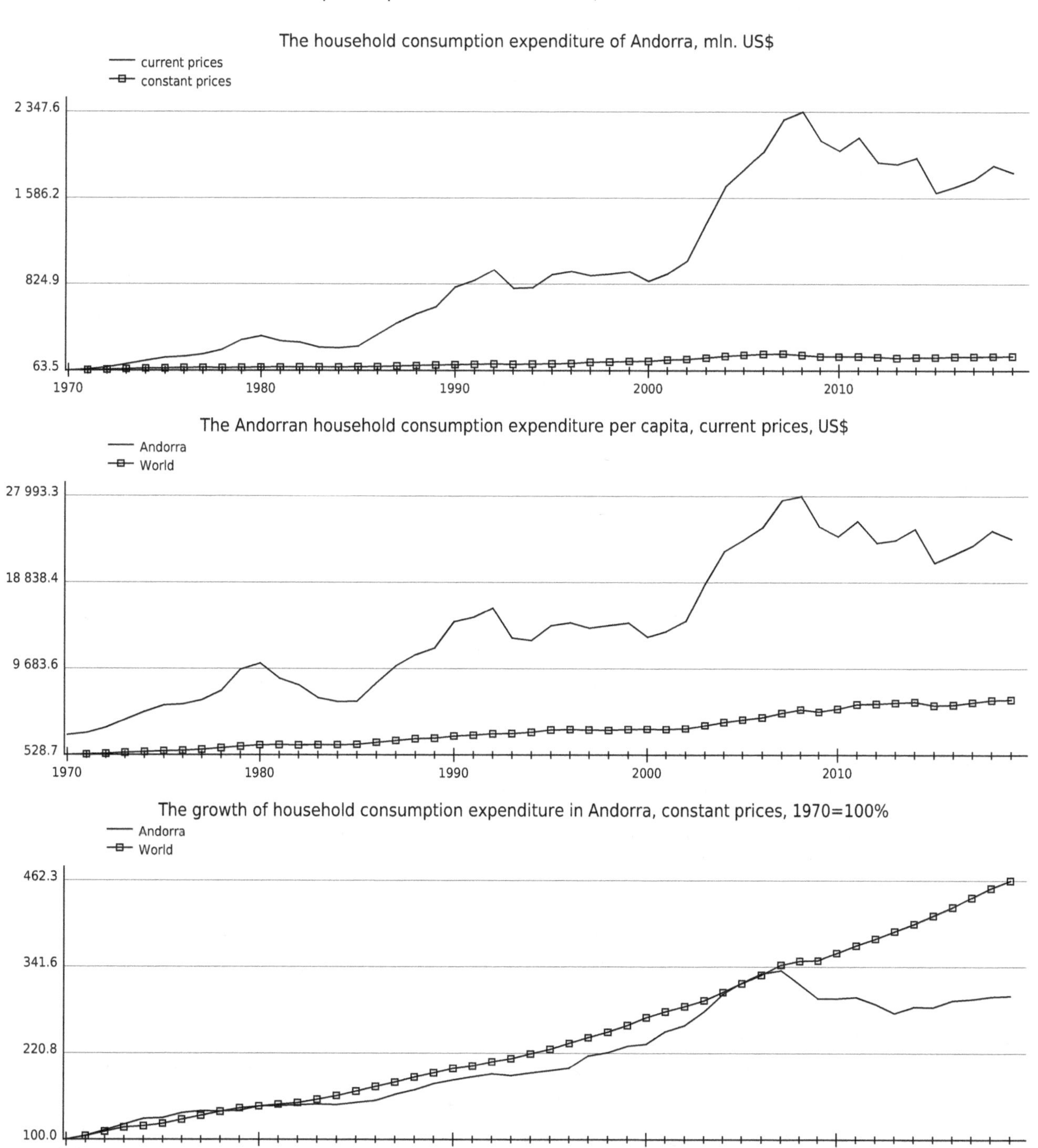

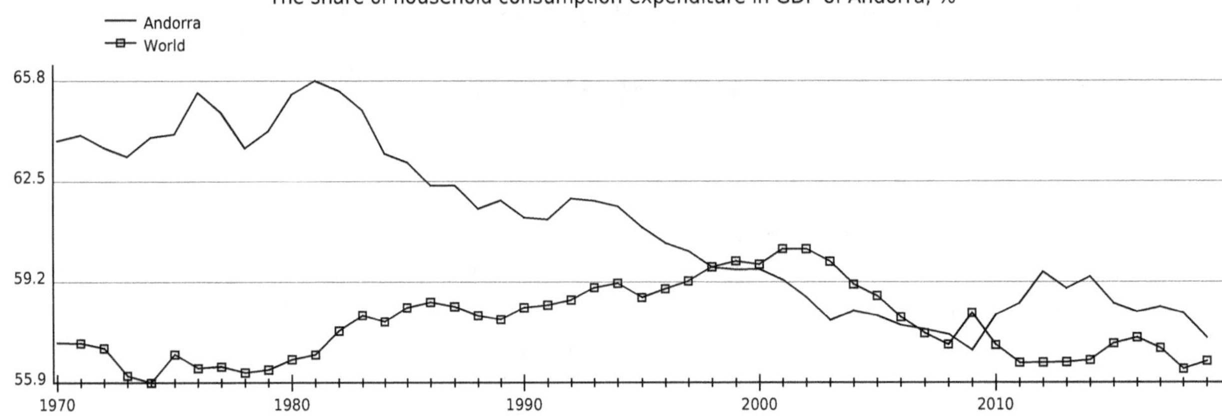

The 1970s

The household consumption expenditure of Andorra was $165.6 million per year in the 1970s, ranked 150th in the world. The share in the world was 0.0045%, and 0.011% in Europe.

The share of household expenditure in GDP of Andorra was 64.2% in the 1970s, ranked 90th in the world, and was on a par with Spain (64.2%), South America (64.3%), Republic of Korea (63.9%).

The Andorran household expenditure per capita was $5 551.3 in the 1970s, ranked 5th in the world. The Andorra's household consumption expenditure per capita was greater than household expenditure per capita in the world ($914.8) in 6.1 times, and was greater than household consumption expenditure per capita in Europe ($2 041.4) in 2.7 times.

The growth of household consumption expenditure in Andorra was 3.8% in the 1970s, ranked 108th in the world, and was on a par with Norway (3.8%), Monaco (3.9%), Hungary (3.9%). The growth of household consumption expenditure in Andorra (3.8%) was less than growth of household consumption expenditure in the world (4.1%), was greater than growth of household expenditure in Europe (3.7%).

Comparison with neighbors. The household expenditure of Andorra was less than in France ($180.7 billion) and in Spain ($68.2 billion). The Andorran household expenditure per capita was greater than in France ($3.4 thousand) and in Spain ($1 913.4). The growth of household consumption expenditure in Andorra was less than in Spain (4.1%) and in France (4.0%).

Comparison with leaders. The Andorran household consumption expenditure was less than in the United States ($1.0 trillion), in the USSR ($310.6 billion), in Japan ($280.9 billion), in Germany ($277.8 billion), and in France ($180.7 billion). The Andorran household expenditure per capita was greater than in the United States ($4.7 thousand), in Germany ($3.5 thousand), in France ($3.4 thousand), in Japan ($2.5 thousand), and in the USSR ($1 231.6). The growth of household expenditure in Andorra was greater than in the USA (3.6%) and in Germany (3.6%); but less than in Japan (5.1%), in the USSR (4.7%), and in France (4.0%).

The 1980s

The Andorra's household expenditure was $386.3 million per year in the 1980s, ranked 151st in the world, and was on a par with Greenland ($392.7 million). The share in the world was 0.0044%, and 0.013% in Europe.

The share of household consumption expenditure in GDP of Andorra was 63.3% in the 1980s, ranked 95th in the world, and was on a par with Spain (63.3%), Tunisia (63.1%), the Caribbean (63.7%).

The Andorra's household consumption expenditure per capita was $8 806.3 in the 1980s, ranked 12th in the world, and was on a par with Norway ($8.9 thousand), Sweden ($8.6 thousand). The household consumption expenditure per capita in Andorra was greater than household expenditure per capita in the world ($1 808.0) in 4.9 times, and was greater than household consumption expenditure per capita in Europe ($3 991.1) in 2.2 times.

The growth of household consumption expenditure in Andorra was 2.4% in the 1980s, ranked 111th in the world, and was on a par with Turkey (2.4%). The growth of household consumption expenditure in Andorra (2.4%) was less than growth of household expenditure in the world (3.0%), was greater than growth of household consumption expenditure in Europe (2.3%).

Comparison with neighbors. The Andorra's household expenditure was less than in France ($408.1 billion) and in Spain ($159.2

billion). The Andorran household consumption expenditure per capita was greater than in France ($7.2 thousand) and in Spain ($4.1 thousand). The growth of household consumption expenditure in Andorra was greater than in France (2.3%) and in Spain (2.3%).

Comparison with leaders. The household expenditure of Andorra was less than in the USA ($2.6 trillion), in Japan ($945.6 billion), in Germany ($575.7 billion), in the USSR ($424.6 billion), and in the UK ($416.5 billion). The household expenditure per capita in Andorra was greater than in Japan ($7.8 thousand), in Germany ($7.4 thousand), in the UK ($7.4 thousand), and in the USSR ($1 542.8); but less than in the United States ($10.9 thousand). The growth of household consumption expenditure in Andorra was greater than in Germany (1.8%); but less than in Japan (3.7%), in the United Kingdom (3.5%), in the USA (3.2%), and in the USSR (3.0%).

The 1990s

The Andorran household consumption expenditure was $878.2 million per year in the 1990s, ranked 165th in the world, and was on a par with the CAR ($869.9 million), Burundi ($868.6 million), Somalia ($868.2 million). The share in the world was 0.0052%, and 0.016% in Europe.

The share of household consumption expenditure in GDP of Andorra was 60.9% in the 1990s, ranked 123rd in the world, and was on a par with Spain (60.9%), South Africa (60.9%), Southern Africa (60.7%).

The household expenditure per capita in Andorra was $14 285.9 in the 1990s, ranked 17th in the world, and was on a par with Austria ($14.3 thousand), the United Arab Emirates ($14.1 thousand), Western Europe ($14.5 thousand). The household consumption expenditure per capita in Andorra was greater than household expenditure per capita in the world ($2 963.9) in 4.8 times, and was greater than household expenditure per capita in Europe ($7 702.2) by 85.5%.

The growth of household consumption expenditure in Andorra was 2.6% in the 1990s, ranked 108th in the world, and was on a par with New Zealand (2.6%), Madagascar (2.6%), Jordan (2.6%). The growth of household consumption expenditure in Andorra (2.6%) was less than growth of household expenditure in the world (3.0%), was greater than growth of household expenditure in Europe (1.8%).

Comparison with neighbors. The Andorra's household consumption expenditure was less than in France ($783.0 billion) and in Spain ($359.2 billion). The Andorran household expenditure per capita was greater than in France ($13.2 thousand) and in Spain ($9.0 thousand). The growth of household expenditure in Andorra was greater than in Spain (2.4%) and in France (1.8%).

Comparison with leaders. The Andorran household consumption expenditure was less than in the USA ($4.9 trillion), in Japan ($2.3 trillion), in Germany ($1.2 trillion), in the UK ($884.5 billion), and in France ($783.0 billion). The Andorran household expenditure per capita was greater than in France ($13.2 thousand); but less than in the United States ($18.5 thousand), in Japan ($18.2 thousand), in the United Kingdom ($15.3 thousand), and in Germany ($15.2 thousand). The growth of household consumption expenditure in Andorra was greater than in Germany (2.1%), in Japan (1.8%), and in France (1.8%); but less than in the United States (3.4%) and in the United Kingdom (2.8%).

The 2000s

The Andorran household consumption expenditure was $1.6 billion per year in the 2000s, ranked 163rd in the world, and was on a par with Guyana ($1.6 billion). The share in the world was 0.0060%, and 0.019% in Europe.

The share of household consumption expenditure in GDP of Andorra was 57.9% in the 2000s, ranked 139th in the world, and was on a par with Spain (57.9%), Northern Europe (58.1%), New Zealand (57.7%).

The household consumption expenditure per capita in Andorra was $21 495.4 in the 2000s, ranked 12th in the world, and was on a par with San Marino ($21.3 thousand), Ireland ($21.2 thousand). The Andorra's household consumption expenditure per capita was greater than household expenditure per capita in the world ($4 208.2) in 5.1 times, and was greater than household expenditure per capita in Europe ($11 901.2) by 80.6%.

The growth of household expenditure in Andorra was 2.6% in the 2000s, ranked 149th in the world, and was on a par with New Caledonia (2.6%), Slovenia (2.6%). The growth of household consumption expenditure in Andorra (2.6%) was less than growth of household consumption expenditure in the world (3.0%), was greater than growth of household consumption expenditure in Europe (2.0%).

Comparison with neighbors. The household expenditure of Andorra was less than in France ($1.1 trillion) and in Spain ($631.3 billion). The Andorran household expenditure per capita was greater than in France ($18.1 thousand) and in Spain ($14.5 thousand). The growth of household consumption expenditure in Andorra was greater than in Spain (2.5%) and in France (2.0%).

Comparison with leaders. The household expenditure of Andorra was less than in the USA ($8.5 trillion), in Japan ($2.6 trillion), in Germany ($1.5 trillion), in the United Kingdom ($1.5 trillion), and in France ($1.1 trillion). The household consumption expenditure per capita in Andorra was greater than in Japan ($20.4 thousand), in Germany ($18.9 thousand), and in France ($18.1 thousand); but less than in the United States ($28.8 thousand) and in the United Kingdom ($25.0 thousand). The growth of household consumption expenditure in Andorra was greater than in the United States (2.4%), in the UK (2.1%), in France (2.0%), in Japan (0.81%), and in Germany (0.46%).

The 2010s

The household expenditure of Andorra was $1.9 billion per year in the 2010s, ranked 169th in the world, and was on a par with Aruba ($1.8 billion). The share in the world was 0.0042%, and 0.016% in Europe.

The share of household expenditure in GDP of Andorra was 58.5% in the 2010s, ranked 137th in the world, and was on a par with Spain (58.5%), India (58.3%), Morocco (58.8%).

The household expenditure per capita in Andorra was $23 321.7 in the 2010s, ranked 21st in the world, and was on a par with Belgium ($23.3 thousand), Japan ($23.4 thousand), New Caledonia ($23.0 thousand). The household consumption expenditure per capita in Andorra was greater than household consumption expenditure per capita in the world ($6 018.5) in 3.9 times, and was greater than household consumption expenditure per capita in Europe ($15 614.2) by 49.4%.

The growth of household consumption expenditure in Andorra was 0.1% in the 2010s, ranked 193rd in the world. The growth of household consumption expenditure in Andorra (0.13%) was less than growth of household expenditure in the world (2.8%), was less than growth of household consumption expenditure in Europe (1.3%).

Comparison with neighbors. The household consumption expenditure of Andorra was 786.0 times lower than in France ($1.5 trillion) and 424.9 times lower than in Spain ($789.9 billion). The household expenditure per capita in Andorra was 5.9% higher than in France ($22.0 thousand) and 38.2% higher than in Spain ($16.9 thousand). The growth of household consumption expenditure in Andorra was less than in France (1.1%) and in Spain (0.45%).

Comparison with leaders. The Andorran household consumption expenditure was 6 558.7 times lower than in the United States ($12.2 trillion), 2 113.8 times lower than in China ($3.9 trillion), 1 607.0 times lower than in Japan ($3.0 trillion), 1 053.5 times lower than in Germany ($2.0 trillion), and 958.6 times lower than in the UK ($1.8 trillion). The Andorran household consumption expenditure per capita was 8.3 times higher than in China ($2.8 thousand); but 38.9% lower than in the USA ($38.2 thousand), 14.1% lower than in the United Kingdom ($27.2 thousand), 2.5% lower than in Germany ($23.9 thousand), and 0.13% lower than in Japan ($23.4 thousand). The growth of household expenditure in Andorra was less than in China (8.3%), in the USA (2.4%), in the United Kingdom (1.8%), in Germany (1.4%), and in Japan (0.64%).

Part V. Reproduction

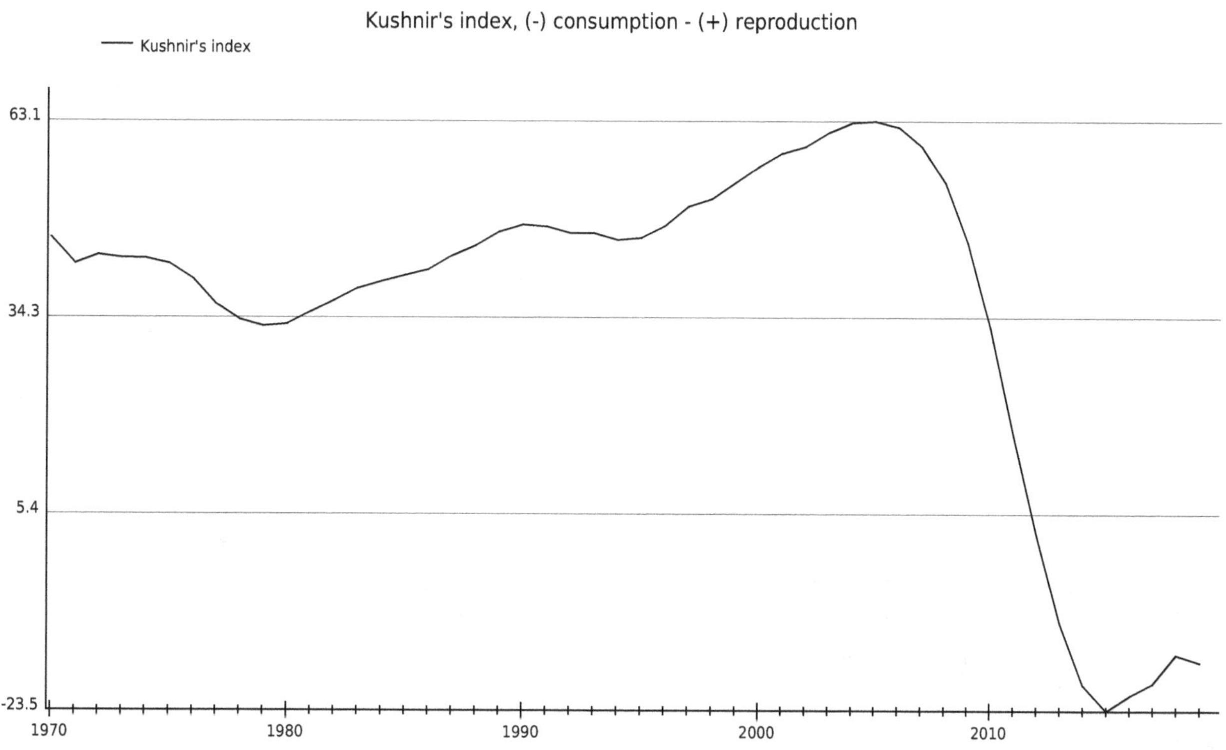

Chapter XIV. Gross fixed capital formation

(including Acquisitions less disposals of valuables)

The fixed capital formation of Andorra rose from $64.8 million per year in the 1970s to $603.8 million per year in the 2010s, that is by $539.0 million or 9.3 times. The change occurred at $481.0 million due to a 4.9-fold increase in prices, as also at -$50.3 million due to a 1.4-fold decrease in per capita rate, as well as at $108.3 million due to the expansion in population. The average annual growth in fixed capital formation is 1.9%. The minimum value of gross fixed capital formation was in 1970 at $26.8 million. The maximum value of fixed capital formation was in 2007 at $1.2 billion.

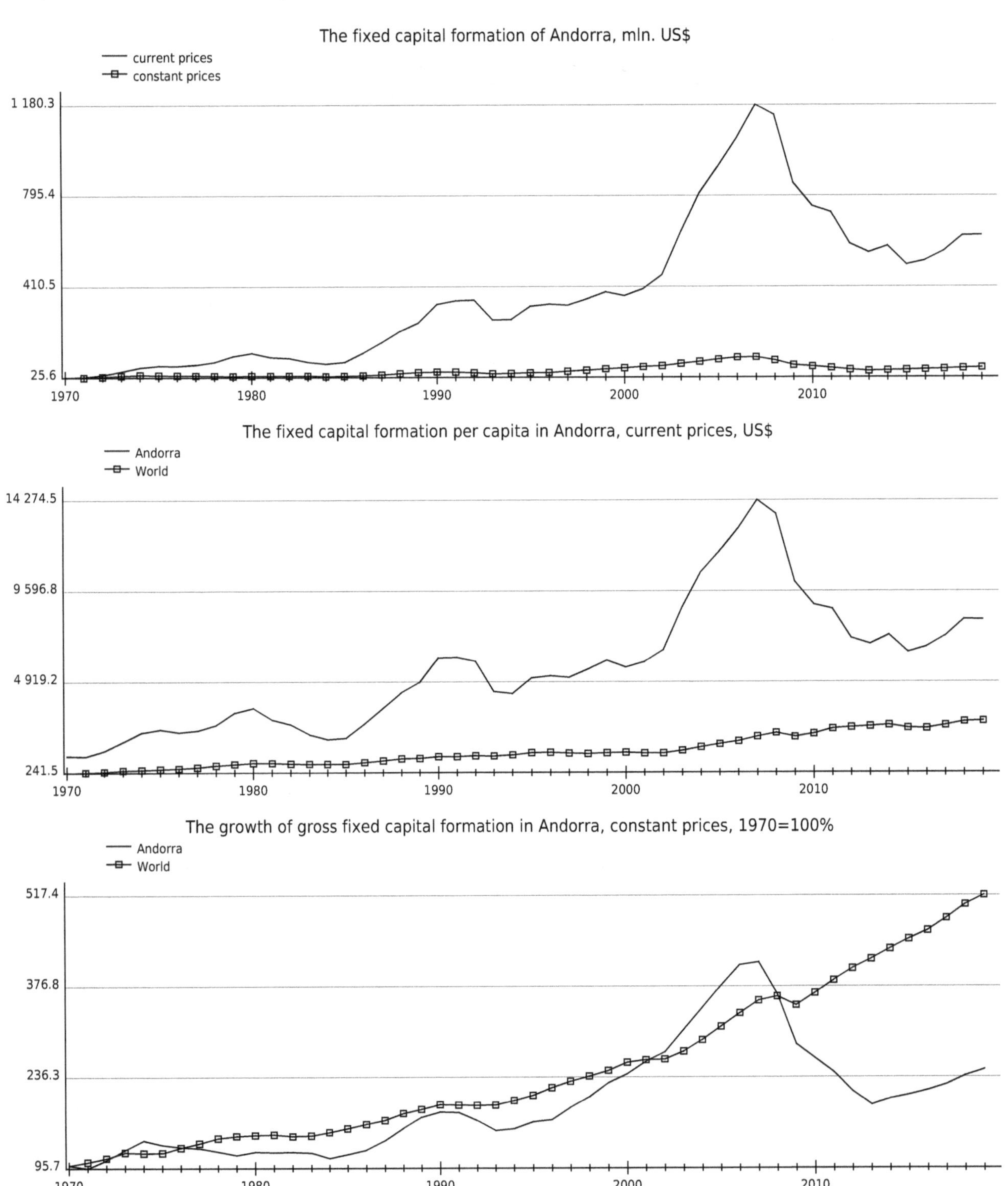

The fixed capital formation of Andorra, mln. US$

The fixed capital formation per capita in Andorra, current prices, US$

The growth of gross fixed capital formation in Andorra, constant prices, 1970=100%

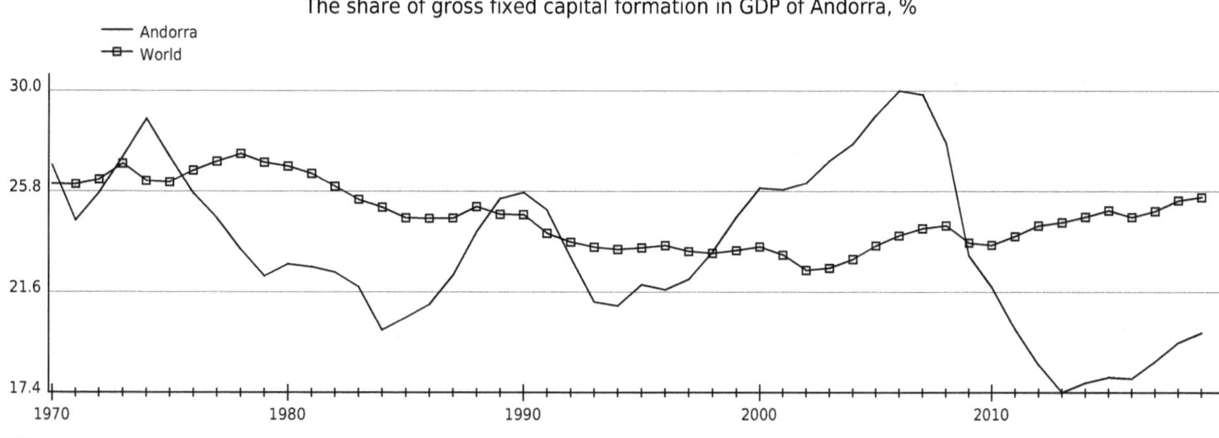

The 1970s

The gross fixed capital formation of Andorra was $64.8 million per year in the 1970s, ranked 146th in the world. The share in the world was 0.0037%, and 0.0088% in Europe.

The share of gross fixed capital formation in GDP of Andorra was 25.1% in the 1970s, ranked 73rd in the world, and was on a par with Spain (25.1%), Italy (25.1%), San Marino (25.0%).

The fixed capital formation per capita in Andorra was $2 172.1 in the 1970s, ranked 9th in the world, and was on a par with Luxembourg ($2.1 thousand). The Andorra's gross fixed capital formation per capita was greater than gross fixed capital formation per capita in the world ($433.5) in 5.0 times, and was greater than gross fixed capital formation per capita in Europe ($1 018.0) in 2.1 times.

The growth of fixed capital formation in Andorra was 1.6% in the 1970s, ranked 153rd in the world. The growth of fixed capital formation in Andorra (1.6%) was less than growth of gross fixed capital formation in the world (4.2%), was less than growth of fixed capital formation in Europe (2.4%).

Comparison with neighbors. The fixed capital formation of Andorra was less than in France ($82.9 billion) and in Spain ($26.7 billion). The fixed capital formation per capita in Andorra was greater than in France ($1 545.4) and in Spain ($748.7). The growth of gross fixed capital formation in Andorra was less than in France (2.7%) and in Spain (1.7%).

Comparison with leaders. The fixed capital formation of Andorra was less than in the United States ($381.9 billion), in the USSR ($214.6 billion), in Japan ($191.6 billion), in Germany ($125.8 billion), and in France ($82.9 billion). The Andorra's fixed capital formation per capita was greater than in the United States ($1 750.0), in Japan ($1 720.7), in Germany ($1 597.2), in France ($1 545.4), and in the USSR ($850.9). The growth of fixed capital formation in Andorra was greater than in Germany (1.5%); but less than in the USA (4.4%), in Japan (3.9%), in the USSR (3.2%), and in France (2.7%).

The 1980s

The Andorra's gross fixed capital formation was $138.8 million per year in the 1980s, ranked 142nd in the world, and was on a par with Aruba ($138.5 million), Greenland ($137.2 million). The share in the world was 0.0036%, and 0.010% in Europe.

The share of fixed capital formation in GDP of Andorra was 22.7% in the 1980s, ranked 79th in the world, and was on a par with Spain (22.7%), Dominica (22.7%), Western Asia (22.7%).

The Andorran fixed capital formation per capita was $3 164.8 in the 1980s, ranked 20th in the world, and was on a par with Denmark ($3.2 thousand), Western Europe ($3.1 thousand), Bahrain ($3.1 thousand). The fixed capital formation per capita in Andorra was greater than gross fixed capital formation per capita in the world ($790.9) in 4.0 times, and was greater than gross fixed capital formation per capita in Europe ($1 748.4) by 81.0%.

The growth of gross fixed capital formation in Andorra was 4.2% in the 1980s, ranked 62nd in the world, and was on a par with Switzerland (4.2%), Bangladesh (4.2%). The growth of fixed capital formation in Andorra (4.2%) was greater than growth of fixed capital formation in the world (2.5%), was greater than growth of gross fixed capital formation in Europe (2.2%).

Comparison with neighbors. The Andorran gross fixed capital formation was less than in France ($164.3 billion) and in Spain ($57.2

billion). The Andorra's gross fixed capital formation per capita was greater than in France ($2.9 thousand) and in Spain ($1 483.8). The growth of fixed capital formation in Andorra was greater than in France (2.4%); but less than in Spain (4.7%).

Comparison with leaders. The Andorra's fixed capital formation was less than in the United States ($958.4 billion), in Japan ($571.7 billion), in the USSR ($271.0 billion), in Germany ($238.1 billion), and in France ($164.3 billion). The Andorra's gross fixed capital formation per capita was greater than in Germany ($3.1 thousand), in France ($2.9 thousand), and in the USSR ($984.8); but less than in Japan ($4.7 thousand) and in the USA ($4.0 thousand). The growth of fixed capital formation in Andorra was greater than in the USA (3.1%), in France (2.4%), in the USSR (1.7%), and in Germany (1.4%); but less than in Japan (4.8%).

The 1990s

The Andorran fixed capital formation was $331.7 million per year in the 1990s, ranked 152nd in the world, and was on a par with Cambodia ($339.8 million). The share in the world was 0.0049%, and 0.015% in Europe.

The share of gross fixed capital formation in GDP of Andorra was 23.0% in the 1990s, ranked 88th in the world, and was on a par with Spain (23.0%), Western Europe (23.0%), Bahrain (23.0%).

The gross fixed capital formation per capita in Andorra was $5 395.3 in the 1990s, ranked 22nd in the world, and was on a par with Finland ($5.4 thousand), the British Virgin Islands ($5.3 thousand), Belgium ($5.3 thousand). The Andorran gross fixed capital formation per capita was greater than fixed capital formation per capita in the world ($1 183.8) in 4.6 times, and was greater than fixed capital formation per capita in Europe ($2 956.1) by 82.5%.

The growth of gross fixed capital formation in Andorra was 2.7% in the 1990s, ranked 115th in the world, and was on a par with Nigeria (2.7%), Indonesia (2.7%), Antigua and Barbuda (2.7%). The growth of gross fixed capital formation in Andorra (2.7%) was less than growth of fixed capital formation in the world (2.8%), was greater than growth of gross fixed capital formation in Europe (0.024%).

Comparison with neighbors. The Andorran gross fixed capital formation was less than in France ($299.3 billion) and in Spain ($135.6 billion). The fixed capital formation per capita in Andorra was greater than in France ($5.0 thousand) and in Spain ($3.4 thousand). The growth of gross fixed capital formation in Andorra was greater than in France (1.5%); but less than in Spain (3.2%).

Comparison with leaders. The gross fixed capital formation of Andorra was less than in the USA ($1.6 trillion), in Japan ($1.3 trillion), in Germany ($520.7 billion), in France ($299.3 billion), and in the United Kingdom ($250.0 billion). The fixed capital formation per capita in Andorra was greater than in France ($5.0 thousand) and in the UK ($4.3 thousand); but less than in Japan ($10.4 thousand), in Germany ($6.5 thousand), and in the USA ($6.1 thousand). The growth of gross fixed capital formation in Andorra was greater than in Germany (2.4%), in the UK (1.7%), in France (1.5%), and in Japan (0.18%); but less than in the USA (4.8%).

The 2000s

The Andorran fixed capital formation was $779.7 million per year in the 2000s, ranked 153rd in the world, and was on a par with Bermuda ($794.4 million). The share in the world was 0.0071%, and 0.023% in Europe.

The share of gross fixed capital formation in GDP of Andorra was 27.5% in the 2000s, ranked 46th in the world, and was on a par with Lesotho (27.5%), Spain (27.5%), Kazakhstan (27.3%).

The Andorran gross fixed capital formation per capita was $10 217.4 in the 2000s, ranked 12th in the world, and was on a par with Denmark ($10.2 thousand), the British Virgin Islands ($10.1 thousand). The Andorran gross fixed capital formation per capita was greater than gross fixed capital formation per capita in the world ($1 690.7) in 6.0 times, and was greater than fixed capital formation per capita in Europe ($4 590.9) in 2.2 times.

The growth of gross fixed capital formation in Andorra was 2.3% in the 2000s, ranked 137th in the world, and was on a par with the Dominican Republic (2.3%), Sweden (2.3%). The growth of fixed capital formation in Andorra (2.3%) was less than growth of fixed capital formation in the world (3.5%), was greater than growth of gross fixed capital formation in Europe (1.6%).

Comparison with neighbors. The Andorran fixed capital formation was less than in France ($463.9 billion) and in Spain ($299.2 billion). The Andorra's fixed capital formation per capita was greater than in France ($7.4 thousand) and in Spain ($6.8 thousand). The growth of gross fixed capital formation in Andorra was greater than in Spain (2.1%) and in France (1.6%).

Comparison with leaders. The fixed capital formation of Andorra was less than in the United States ($2.8 trillion), in Japan ($1.2 trillion), in China ($1.0 trillion), in Germany ($557.7 billion), and in France ($463.9 billion). The Andorra's fixed capital formation per capita was greater than in the USA ($9.4 thousand), in Japan ($9.0 thousand), in France ($7.4 thousand), in Germany ($6.9 thousand), and in China ($782.2). The growth of gross fixed capital formation in Andorra was greater than in France (1.6%), in the United States (0.43%), in Germany (-0.56%), and in Japan (-2.0%); but less than in China (13.4%).

The 2010s

The fixed capital formation of Andorra was $603.8 million per year in the 2010s, ranked 175th in the world, and was on a par with Djibouti ($605.7 million). The share in the world was 0.0031%, and 0.014% in Europe.

The share of fixed capital formation in GDP of Andorra was 19.0% in the 2010s, ranked 158th in the world, and was on a par with Spain (19.0%), Iraq (19.0%), Kuwait (19.1%).

The Andorra's fixed capital formation per capita was $7 575.6 in the 2010s, ranked 36th in the world. The fixed capital formation per capita in Andorra was greater than fixed capital formation per capita in the world ($2 621.1) in 2.9 times, and was greater than fixed capital formation per capita in Europe ($5 775.6) by 31.2%.

The growth of fixed capital formation in Andorra was -1.4% in the 2010s, ranked 186th in the world. The growth of fixed capital formation in Andorra (-1.4%) was less than growth of fixed capital formation in the world (4.1%), was less than growth of fixed capital formation in Europe (2.2%).

Comparison with neighbors. The Andorra's gross fixed capital formation was 993.3 times lower than in France ($599.8 billion) and 424.8 times lower than in Spain ($256.5 billion). The Andorran gross fixed capital formation per capita was 38.3% higher than in Spain ($5.5 thousand); but 16.2% lower than in France ($9.0 thousand). The growth of fixed capital formation in Andorra was less than in France (1.9%) and in Spain (0.13%).

Comparison with leaders. The Andorra's fixed capital formation was 7 489.9 times lower than in China ($4.5 trillion), 5 960.2 times lower than in the United States ($3.6 trillion), 2 004.2 times lower than in Japan ($1.2 trillion), 1 246.2 times lower than in Germany ($752.5 billion), and 1 153.9 times lower than in India ($696.8 billion). The fixed capital formation per capita in Andorra was 2.3 times higher than in China ($3.2 thousand) and 14.2 times higher than in India ($535.2); but 32.7% lower than in the USA ($11.3 thousand), 19.9% lower than in Japan ($9.5 thousand), and 17.6% lower than in Germany ($9.2 thousand). The growth of gross fixed capital formation in Andorra was less than in China (8.0%), in India (5.8%), in the United States (3.8%), in Germany (2.8%), and in Japan (1.8%).